Andha Yug

It is the last day of the Mahabharata war: the city is burning, Kurukshetra is covered with the dead, and only a few Kauravas survive. Egged on by the Kauravas, Ashwatthama releases the *brahmastra,* the ultimate weapon which threatens to destroy the world. And Krishna—the embodiment of compassion, truth, and justice—is cursed by the Kauravas for causing the war.

One of the most significant plays of post-Independence India, Dharamvir Bharati's *Andha Yug* continues to raise pertinent moral and political issues, and has become all the more relevant in a terrorized rift-stricken twenty-first century.

'*Andha Yug* is one of the great Indian plays of the last millennium, and in Alok Bhalla it has found an ideal translator. He is sensitive to the complex tensions swirling within its epic edifice, not afraid to enhance its muted nuances where necessary, or to go for a risky option when the choices are unclear. Bhalla's *Andha Yug* is a model in the fraught field of translation.'

—Girish Karnad, playwright, Padma Bhushan
and Jnanpith Laureate

'Dharamvir Bharati's *Andha Yug* is a landmark in the history of Hindi drama. Alok Bhalla's fine translation is austere and rigorous, negotiating as it does, both the dimensions of the play—its epic scale and the Spartan simplicity of its poetry.'

—Keki N. Daruwalla, poet, Sahitya Akademi Laureate

'*Andha Yug* is one of the most compelling meditations written in and about the dark time following Partition. Alok Bhalla's masterful translation captures beautifully the resonance and subtlety of the play's argument. Bhalla has done for Bharati what the great English translators of recent years—Lattimore, Fitzgerald, and Fagles—accomplished for Homer's Greek epics: a rendering in measured yet forceful English poetry the ecstatic temptation of both good and evil, and the sacred ground between them.'

—Frank Stewart, Professor, University of Hawaii,
and Editor, *Manoa*

Andha Yug

DHARAMVIR BHARATI

Translated, with a Critical Introduction, by
ALOK BHALLA

OXFORD
UNIVERSITY PRESS

OXFORD
UNIVERSITY PRESS

Oxford University Press is a department of the University of Oxford.
It furthers the University's objective of excellence in research, scholarship,
and education by publishing worldwide. Oxford is a registered trademark of
Oxford University Press in the UK and in certain other countries

Published in India by
Oxford University Press
22 Workspace, 2nd Floor, 1/22 Asaf Ali Road, New Delhi 110002, India

First Edition published in 2005
Oxford India Paperbacks 2010
25th impression 2024

ISBN-13: 978-0-19-806522-7
ISBN-10: 0-19-806522-1

Typeset in Bembo 10/12
by Sai Graphic Design, New Delhi
Printed in India by Rakmo Press Pvt. Ltd

MR. Omayal Achi MR. Arunachalam Trust was set up in 1976 to further education
and health care particularly in rural areas. The MR. AR. Educational Society was
later established by the Trust. One of the Society's activities is to sponsor Indian
literature. This translation is entirely bound by the MR. AR. Educational Society
as part of its aims.

*This translation
is for
our two daughters
Udita
and
Damini*

Contents

Defending the Sacred in an Age of Atrocities
On Translating *Andha Yug*

Alok Bhalla

My decision to translate Dharamvir Bharati's *Andha Yug* (1953) was the result of whimsy of course, but whimsy in the service of practical reason, and, given the present condition of the country, in the aid of political sanity too. I spent a semester teaching a course on contemporary Indian theatre, with the help of English translations which were mostly bad. Strangely enough, *Andha Yug,* which was so literally translated as to seem like a long poem without any distinguishable theatrical or moral voices at all, and so thoughtlessly edited as to confuse any good logician, became the focus of rather disturbing discussions about the politics of revenge, the impotence of grief, the meaning of *karuna,* the failure of a morally responsible will to intervene in acts of violation, and the responsibility of the gods in leading us to moral dereliction and decay.[1] Nearly every student pitied Gandhari, and there was unanimous condemnation of Krishna. Krishna made them uncomfortable—He should have behaved more like a dissembling politician pretending to fulfil our needs and wishes, rights and demands so as to win our votes, instead of acting like a god on behalf of morality and justice. Gandhari, they felt, was right in making Ashwatthama the invincible instrument of her revenge against the Pandavas. She had a greater moral claim to our sympathy than Krishna, whose omnipotence should have alerted him to his responsibilities and, thereby, helped the Pandavas and the Kauravas evade a catastrophic war by transforming them into moral visionaries.

My students, I must insist, were not more ethically obtuse than any of us. After all, we all demand that gods behave like highly-paid *karamcharis* or non-government officers, look after our social and physical hygiene, be alert to all our psychological anxieties, and protest on our behalf against caste, gender, or class wrongs, instead of bearing witness to the

---

[1] *Andha Yug* was first translated by Paul Jacob as *The Blind Age.* It was published in *Enact,* No. 65, May 1972.

causes of grief, or marking out places of evil in our souls, and, sometimes, even singing praises for acts which are *just* so as to save that fragile thing called hope. Maybe, if we are more charitable, we think that God is no more than a junior judge in the lower court, where 'arid disputes'[2] are sorted out, instead of being the very form and idea of the good, which finds its earthly incarnation in acts of knowledge, work, and love when they are performed with the full absorbedness of the soul.

Talking to my students about the moral issues raised by *Andha Yug*, I recalled what the great Jewish philosopher, Martin Buber, who had corresponded with Mahatma Gandhi about the ethics of non-violent resistance against a ruthless enemy,[3] had rightly said when he asserted that thinking about God was unavoidable in times of atrocities. Without invoking an absolute notion of the good or the just, all our truth-seeking impulses, especially when our very existence as a people is threatened, can only flounder and fall into nothingness. Thinking about what could be absolute and unconditional for human survival during the years of the holocaust in Germany, years which coincided with the holocaust during the partition of India, he felt, as perhaps Dharamvir Bharati did, that no other 'word of human speech is so misused, so defiled, so desecrated'[4] as the word 'God'. Yet, Buber insisted, as I think Bharati does in the play, that in times of extreme violence the word 'God' needs to be defended with passion, for our sense of ourselves as human beings depends upon it. Buber's case for holding on to the word 'God' is moving and eloquent:

Yes, it [God] is the most heavy-laden of all human words. None has become so soiled, so mutilated. Just for this reason I may not abandon it. Generations of men have laid the burden of their anxious lives upon this word ... it lies in the dust and bears their whole burden. The races of man with their religious factions have torn the word to pieces; they have killed for it and died for it, and it bears their finger marks and their blood. Where might I find a word like it to describe the highest! If I took the purest, most sparkling concept from the inner treasure-chamber of the philosophers ... I could not capture the presence of Him whom generations of men have honoured and degraded with their awesome living

[2] W. H. Auden, 'In Memory of Sigmund Freud', *Collected Shorter Poems* (New York: Random House, 1964), p. 169.

[3] For Buber's letters to Gandhi see *Pointing the Way*, trans. Maurice Friedman (London: Routledge and Kegan Paul, 1957), pp. 126–47.

[4] Quoted by Iris Murdoch in *Metaphysics as a Guide to Morals* (London: Penguin, 1992), p. 420.

and dying. I do indeed mean Him whom hell-tormented and heaven-storming generations of men mean. Certainly, they draw caricatures and write 'God' underneath; they murder one another and say 'in God's name'. But when all the madness and delusion fall to dust, when they stand over against Him in the loneliest darkness and no longer say 'He, He', but rather sigh 'Thou', shout 'Thou' ... and when they then add 'God', is it not the real God whom they all implore, the One Living God, the God of the children of man? Is it not He who *hears* them? And just for this reason is not the word 'God,' the word of appeal, the word which has become a *name*, consecrated in all human tongues for all time? We must esteem those who interdict it because they rebel against the injustice and wrong which are so readily referred to 'God' for authorisation. But we must not give up. How understandable it is that some suggest that we should remain silent about the 'last things' for a time in order that the misused words may be redeemed! But they are not to be redeemed *thus*. We cannot cleanse the word 'God' and we cannot make it whole; but, defiled and mutilated as it is, we can raise it from the ground and set it over an hour of great care. (Quoted by Murdoch, pp. 420-1).

Buber's God is the difficult and demanding Judaic God who is utterly remote, totally transcendent, yet ever watchful over human affairs. His presence, Buber insists, is essential for the survival of the soul in the conditions of extremity in which much of the twentieth century has been lived.

In contrast, Bharati's Krishna, though equally firm and ruthless in his moral judgements, is a more humanly-cherished figure, with whom the self can always conduct a dialogue. Because Krishna's presence does not produce fear and trembling, he can be chastised and cursed, loved and worshipped, abandoned and killed. Indeed, it is not surprising that, in the play, an ordinary man can set himself up as Krishna's brother and, acting as the keeper of Krishna's faith, chastise him for violations of the law. Balarama can, thus, tell Krishna:

> Say what you like, Krishna
> But what Bhima did today
> violated dharma.
> His attack
> was an act
> of betrayal ...
> The Pandavas are related to us
> but are the Kauravas our enemies?
> I would have confronted Bhima today

but you stopped me.
I have known you since childhood.
You have always been
an unprincipled rogue![5]

It is interesting to note that here, as elsewhere in the play, Krishna is neither seen nor heard. The Kaurava soldiers, who overhear Balarama, are delighted by his enraged condemnation of Krishna because it echoes their own blinding rage at their defeat. Krishna's replies fail to penetrate the noise of their own blustering and singleminded conviction about the rightness of their belief that power or might can always be translated into justice. Indeed, what alienates the Kauravas from our sympathy throughout the Mahabharata is their inability to imagine the infinite variety of ways in which the good manifests itself in the ordinary world and which may be the reality of Krishna. Like hundreds of Kaurava souls, we are tempted into believing that ambition, mockery, and the palaces of glass are more worthy of all our efforts than accepting the grace of thinking about and seeking the good. Like the Kauravas, we invariably refuse to hear the voice of God and blame him when our ambitions are not fulfilled; refuse, like the Kauravas in the play, to gaze inwards and find within the sources of grievous wrong.

Yet, while teaching *Andha Yug*, my sympathies were with my students, who responded with such rage against Krishna in the play because, after all, it is easier to ask what God ought to do for us than to consider what we can do for God so that he searches for us.[6] Unlike Buber's God, who is 'elsewhere' and, thus, remote from the most contingent of human concerns and immune from our commonest judgements, Krishna is a more complex figure to deal with. His very human presence makes us demand that his actions and judgements support our present and relative interests or suit our contemporary style of functioning, and when he fails to endorse our ordinary desires, we turn away from him as if he is the reason for our guilty actions and the cause of our sorrows.

The existing translations also misdirected the attention of my students. They captured the shrill voices of pain effectively, but erased the difficult cadences of speech and muted the voices of moral anxiety of characters like Vidura, Sanjaya, and Yuyutsu, drowning them in the clash of armour and steel. Our moral difficulties were compounded by the fact that the

[5] The English translations from the play, here and elsewhere, are mine.
[6] The idea is taken from Simone Weil's *Waiting for God*, trans. Emma Craufurd (New York: Harper and Row, 1951).

two crucial scenes in which Krishna made his presence felt through small, gentle, and loving things, like the feather of a peacock or the sound of a flute or the music of bells ringing in the midst of desolation, were allowed to pass by as of little consequence so that we could get on with the real business of listening to the voices of the defeated shouting for revenge.

Given the intensity of the moral anxieties *Andha Yug* evoked, it was obvious that the play, written soon after the carnage of the partition of the Indian subcontinent, which nearly erased a form of life and civilization, and being read once again in our *rakshas* times of hysterical unreason, still had the power to make us realize how close we live to the borders of nightmares.

Unfortunately, however, the existing translations were not so finely inflected as to help us understand whether the play was about our anguish at finding ourselves in a terrible world where we could only lament and curse, or whether it invited us to hear, in its difficult notes of tragedy, our own complicity in evil. For a majority of my students, it was the gods who made the lives of Gandhari, Dhritarashtra, Duryodhana, and Ashwatthama so bitter, this suggested that the translations had failed to guide their moral attention along the pilgrim path of truth, a path that Vidura and Yudhishthira never abandon in the play even in the midst of carnage. The translations, it was apparent, had not been undertaken after a critical analysis of the play. Not surprising, therefore, my students had failed to notice that the decisive events in the play, which had opened an abyss before the Kauravas, had nothing to do with supernatural forces seeking victims for their perverse delight. In Act I, for instance, Vidura reminds Dhritarashtra that, years before the war, his councillors had warned the Kauravas about the fate of kingdoms which refuse to abide by the laws of truth:

DHRITARASHTRA: Vidura
for the first time
in my life
I am afraid.

VIDURA: Afraid?
The fear you experience today
had gripped others years ago.

DHRITARASHTRA: Why didn't you warn me then?

VIDURA: Bhishma did.
So did Dronacharya.

Indeed, in this very court
Krishna advised you:
   'Do not violate the code of honour.
   If you violate the code of honour
   it will coil around the Kaurava clan
   like a wounded python
   and crush it like a dry twig'....

Yet from the very first day
it was obvious that the Kaurava might
—the final arbiter of truth—
was weak and vulnerable.

Over the past seventeen days
you have received news
of the death
—one by one—
of the entire Kaurava clan.

Vidura is right in insisting that virtue is not a utilitarian service which can be called in to help when we are in trouble and forgotten about at other times. A moral life demands perpetual attention. And those, like Dhritarashtra, who fail to understand this, cannot hope to escape the consequences. In the balance of things, then, it is right that, at the end of all the carnage which he had failed to prevent, Dhritarashtra is consumed by a relentless forest fire, a manifestation of the desolation and the affliction of his soul.

The existing translations of *Andha Yug* had erased the distinctions in moral perceptions, which were carefully structured in the original Hindi text. They had also failed to separate the different levels of ethical awareness available to all human beings, so as to show why some characters, even those like Gandhari, whose suffering saturates us with pity, deserve their fate because they were actually responsible for the breakdown of the moral order and their own ruin with it. The original version of the play in Hindi clarifies repeatedly, sometimes through Vidura's moral commentary and at other times through choric interventions, why it was neither Krishna's hardness of heart, nor his political cunning, nor his amoral opportunism which made him insist that Karna and Duryodhana be killed ruthlessly. It also explains why he curses Ashwatthama to wander through the endless wastes of time.

Karna, for instance, chooses to live with the Kauravas out of his mistaken notions of gratitude, faithfulness, and duty. He realizes, too late, that he had relied merely on armed might to protect him. It was not surprising, therefore, that when the forces of the Kauravas crumble, he finds himself standing in the mud beside his broken chariot, helpless, disabled, and unarmed. What more can he teach us? As he shouts for fairness in frustrated rage, we are required to understand that power without the imagination of mercy can only lead to humiliation. Why should he continue to live after that? And why should not Krishna condone all means available to destroy him? The sacred, after all, is not required to make sentimental compromises when it comes to restoring the just balance of the world in which we live. In the face of an annihilating power, the sacred may use all the available ruthlessness that it can muster up in order to survive. We may, in our mistaken and fallen world, accuse the sacred of hard-heartedness. But, how else will we sometimes learn that there are limits of *adharma* and *atyachar* beyond which we may not go without inviting the wrath of the sacred?

Similarly, in Bharati's play, Duryodhana has to experience the shame of fear before his death for he had not understood it sufficiently when he had Draupadi stripped in court. There can be no consolation for him as he slides behind some watery reeds trying to hide from his fate, and is then crushed to death by Bhima—the coarse and brutal face of justice that sometimes must be revealed. That is why the description of his defeat in the battlefield in Act Three, given to us quite appropriately by Ashwatthama whose understanding of the moral issues of the war is deficient, fills us with terror, but does not touch us with pity. This is how Ashwatthama describes Duryodhana's death to Gandhari—his voice marked with uncomprehending rage and contempt for the Pandavas:

> The Pandava sense of honour
> was on display today
> when Bhima
> violating all the codes of war
> threw Duryodhana down
> smashed his thighs
> broke his arms and his neck.
>
> And then
> with his foot on Duryodhana's head
> Bhima stood on him with all his weight
> and roared like a wild beast!
> The veins on Duryodhana's head

swelled and suddenly burst.
He screamed in pain.
His broken legs jerked.
He opened his eyes
and looked at his people.

As we hear this account of his death, we must, if we don't want our souls to corrode by seeming to relish such violence, stand beside Gandhari as she weeps over his death. But we must not, for the sake of our rational well-being, approve when she curses Krishna for her son's death and asserts that Duryodhana's victory would have been the triumph of dharma.

Duryodhana's miserable fate should, instead, remind us that he had erased the pledge to a minimum ethicality we must all make in our daily lives, so that we do not act with crass stupidity in our encounters with the world. Till the end, Duryodhana fails to see that he himself is responsible for the extreme perversion of life that war represents. There is justice in the fact that he dies unconsoled, cursing Krishna. Words of repentance from him would only have added another untruth to the world. His fanaticism has to be isolated and identified as the cause of suffering. 'Thus it is,' as Simone Weil says, 'that those whom destiny lends might perish for having relied too much upon it.'[7]

Duryodhana and Karna are, however, only a part of the argument, the moral imagery of the play, and not the primary concern of its theatrical narrative. The action of the play takes place on the last night of the Mahabharata war and is centred on the plight of a few bewildered survivors of the Kaurava clan—Gandhari, Dhritarashtra, Ashwatthama, and a handful of others. The ramparts are in ruins, the city is burning, and Kurukshetra is covered with corpses and vultures. The ordinary foot-soldiers of the Kaurava army are cynical about those who control the affairs of state. They are more concerned about their immediate physical survival than about questions of law or virtue. Besides, they know that dynasties change and fall, and that it is more prudent for people like themselves to stand by the rampart walls and wait for the next ruler who needs their services and is willing to pay for them.

GUARD 1:   Honour!

---

[7] 'The "Iliad", Poem of Might,' in *Intimations of Christianity among the Ancient Greeks* (1957; reprint London: Arc, 1987), p. 34.

GUARD 2:   Disbelief!

GUARD 1:   Sorrow at the death of one's sons!

GUARD 2:   The future that is waiting to be born!

GUARD 1:   All these
            grace the lives of kings!

GUARD 2:   And the one they worship as their Lord
            takes responsibility for all of them!

GUARD 1:   But what about the lives
            the two of us have spent
            in these desolate corridors?

GUARD 2:   Who shall take
            responsibility for us?

GUARD 1:   We did not violate honour
            because we did not have any.

GUARD 2:   We were never tormented by disbelief
            because we never had any faith.

GUARD 1:   We never experienced any sorrow.

GUARD 1:   nor felt any pain.

GUARD 2:   We spent our desolate lives
            in these desolate corridors.

GUARD 1:   because we were only slaves.

GUARD 2:   We merely followed the orders of a blind king.

GUARD 1:   We had no opinions of our own.
            we made no choices

GUARD 2:   That is why
            from the beginning
            we have paced these desolate corridors
            from right to left

and then from left to right
without any meaning
without any purpose.

GUARD 2:   Even after death
                we shall pace
                the desolate corridors
                of death's kingdom
                from right to left
                and then from left to right.

The other survivors, the ones who have invested the war with heroic
arguments, are overwhelmed by grief and rage. They have lived for so
long in *tamas* that they fail to notice how close they are to annihilation.
Morally blind, they cannot turn away from egotism, give up their
fascination with power, recognize that others too have suffered, and stop
longing for overwhelming vengeance which will redeem them.
Ashwatthama, for instance, blinded by his passion for revenge, says:

I shall live
like a blind and ruthless beast
and may
Dharmaraj's prophecy come true!

Let both my hands
turn into claws!
Let these eyes
sharp like the teeth of a carnivore
tear the body
of anyone they see!

From now on
my only dharma is;
    'Kill, kill, kill
    and kill again!'

Let that be
the final purpose
of my existence!

We sympathize with the assumption of the remaining members of
the Kaurava clan that a battlefield is the harshest of places anywhere, and

that the only choices which matter there are strategic ones which can ensure survival or victory. That is why the survivors quibble about violations of the laws of war. They think that Krishna should act as a referee, and they curse him when, as the upholder of dharma, he judges them. Since they lose the war, they think it is futile to talk about right or wrong. For them, dharma is not that radical ethicality which a critically alert reason always recognizes, and which could enable them to escape the sorrows and passions of profane time. They continue to debase the idea of dharma, continue to mutilate it, by thinking of it as nothing more than all that satisfies their personal desires in an utterly contingent world. It is not surprising, then, that for the Kaurava survivors, still thirsting for revenge on the last night of the war, Ashwatthama is the only saviour left. Indeed, Ashwatthama embodies what the Kauravas have stood for all along—ambition instead of peace, power instead of companionship, avoidance of responsibility instead of justice, contempt for everything instead of hope for the well-being of all things. One of the terrible ironies of the play is that Gandhari, refusing to understand what kind of monster Ashwatthama really is, removes the bandage from her eyes so as to bless him with her visionary sight and give to his body the adamantine polish of precious stones. All her accumulated grace is wasted as, immediately afterwards, Krishna curses Ashwatthama and transforms his body into a putrid thing. It falls upon Sanjaya, the prophetic narrator whose task it is to tell the truth always, to describe Ashwatthama's physical decay to Gandhari as follows:

SANJAYA: No, no!
He is hideous
his body is rotten
with boils and open sores ...

For the sin of infanticide
Krishna cursed him
with immortality
and condemned him
to live forever and ever.

Cut and slashed by the Lord's disc
his body shall fester forever.
Soiled bandages shall staunch
the blood that shall flow
from his wounds forever and ever.

Lacerated, defiled, filthy, and corrupted
he shall wander
through thick and deep forests
forever and ever.

His body shall be covered with boils
his skin shall rot with pus and scabs
and spittle and phlegm and bile
and he shall live forever and ever.

Excruciating pain will rip
through each limb.

Every bone in his body
will be corroded by suffering
and the Lord shall not let him die.

He will become an abomination
and he shall live forever and ever.

At the end of the play, as he tries to hide from human gaze, Ashwatthama becomes the dramatic correlative of the exhaustion of the ethical. His broken presence signifies that moment in the chronology of a civilization when, in complete despair, it ceases to believe that it has a future. That is why Ashwatthama can contemplate genocide, decide that everyone and everything on earth can be annihilated, and justify his decision to erase all traces of life as the inevitable consequence of the history he has lived. When he releases the 'unthinkable' weapon, the *brahmastra*, he is the monster each of one of us can become when, afraid of losing our selfhood, we dismiss Krishna as a rumour or an opinion, and deny that the ethical must always have a sanctuary in human time.

Yet, throughout the play, as indeed in the Mahabharata, whenever we fear that life is now so accursed that we shall never again see the ordinary world, the Kauravas are given another chance to acknowledge their complicity in evil and turn toward the ethical. Indeed, just as in the Mahabharata, the Gita lies at the heart of the story (I am not concerned about whether it is an interpolation) in *Andha Yug* Krishna's presence, suddenly and unexpectedly, breaks into the narrative of pain—the soft sounds of a flute drift across the battlefield, a peacock feather floats down the ramparts, as if to remind the Kauravas that the sensuous world they, like all human beings, had once longed for still lies just outside the present circle of suffering and needs the grace of justice and truth. And then, as

Gandhari, in her utter mistakenness, curses him for having caused the war, Krishna, like a calm *satyagrahi* (I use this word lest we forget the play was written soon after the genocidal days of the partition when we had abused Gandhi), accepts the curse in the hope of bringing the cycle of violence and revenge to an end. It is terrible to watch her remorse as she realizes the enormity of her fault. She suddenly understands that she has lost the last of the honourable choices it was still possible for the Kauravas to make, and that, henceforth, she can expect no mercy for herself or her clan.

That Krishna, given the chronologies of violence that follow the Mahabharata war, fails to ensure peace is not the fault of the good that he represents, or of the compassionate forms of life he pleads for. In Bharati's play, Krishna is the man of justice and truth we can all become. He is 'the advocate of all created things and their finest embodiment.'[8]

If I am right, then the primary concern of *Andha Yug* is to reveal that the ethical and the sacred that Krishna represents is always available to human beings even in the most atrocious of times. That is why he is at the centre of the play and his abiding presence frames each act of the narrative, during which the surviving Kauravas repeatedly refuse to acknowledge his righteousness and so slide further into moral and spiritual desolation. It is this aspect of Krishna's presence, which so clearly informs the thematic, the poetic, and the structural patterns of the original Hindi play, that is either distorted or ignored in the existing English translations.

Andha Yug is a tragedy that happens because the Kauravas, in their greed, stupidity, and blindness, so disfigure and deny Krishna as to blot out from their social and political vision every possibility of creating cities of virtue and hope. The English translations, on the other hand, make the anguish of Ashwatthama and the sorrow of Gandhari the primary concern of the play. We are so overwhelmed by the knowledge of their suffering that we sympathize with them as victims of forces beyond their control and understanding. Krishna, thus, emerges as a capricious and manipulative god who kills us for his sport—a sentiment that may appeal to our present nausea with everything ethical or sacred, but is surely contrary to Dharamvir Bharati's intention, and, perhaps, not altogether encouraging for those who still dream of making good civil societies.

---

[8] The phrase is taken from Walter Benjamin's, 'The Story-Teller; Reflections on the Works of Nikolai Leskov', *Illuminations*, trans. Harry Zohn (New York: Schoken, 1969), p. 104.

In my translation, I have tried to restore the sacred and the ethical back to the text. I want to ensure that my English translation does not become vulnerable to existentialist anxieties, but retains the play's essential tension between the nightmare of self-enchantment, which the story of the Kauravas represents, and the ever-present possibility of finding an opening out of *tamas* into a redemptive ethicality. My English translation, I hope, shall clearly mark out the fact that the stories of Gandhari and Ashwatthama are nearly always, and in every act, not only countered by different levels of ethical awareness, but are also framed by two different kinds of choric voices. I should like to call the first frame, with which the play actually opens and which is sung as we watch dispirited soldiers drag themselves off the battlefield, 'the chorus of sacred rememorialization'. This choric beginning is made out of fragments taken from Chapter XXIV, Book IV of the *Vishnu Purana* and is meant to be sung in Sanskrit. It asserts that the sacred, which had once manifested itself in the ordinary and the profane world, can always reveal itself in historical time again— that even a battlefield can be the site of hierophany. It should, I think, be possible to convey the sonority of the Puranic song to the English reader by having the English translation follow each separate phrase or *shloka* in Sanskrit.

I should like to call the second chorus that frames the main narrative 'the chorus of ethical lament'. This chorus does two things. It provides a link between the different episodes of the story and, at the same time, voices its moral dismay over the fact that the characters, in their perversity of selfhood, refuse to pay heed to the song of the sacred just heard, and slide further and further toward the blank silence of non-being and nothingness, toward *Andha Yug*. These frames of sacrality and ethicality, however, ensure that, despite human folly, life shall always be granted a ground of mercy below which it will never fall. We are, I think, supposed to remember this even as we watch the story of Gandhari's curse and Ashwatthama's damnation come to an end with the final choric song:

> That day the world descended into the age of darkness
> which has no end, and repeats itself over and over again ...
>
> The age of darkness has seeped into our very souls ...
>
> And yet it is also true
> that like a small seed
> buried somewhere
> in the mind of man

there is courage
and a longing for freedom
and the imagination to create something new.

That seed is buried
without exception
in each of us
and it grows from day to day
in our lives
as duty
as honour
as freedom
as virtuous conduct.

It is this small seed
that makes us fear
half-truths
and great wars
and always
saves
the future of mankind
from blind doubt
slavery
and defeat.

Prefatory Note

Andha Yug would never have been written if it had been in my power not to write it! I was in a dilemma when the idea of writing the play rose within me. It made me a little afraid. I knew that if I set out to write it, I would never be able to turn back!

But, then, there is something called addiction—in accepting the challenge of a roaring sea, fighting the high waves with one's bare hands, plunging down to immeasurable depths, and, then, after facing all the dangers, resurfacing with a few grains of faith, illumination, truth, and dignity—and, this addiction is mingled with such deep agony and so much joy that one can never give it up. *Andha Yug* was written to satisfy that addiction.

After reaching a certain stage one is no longer afraid. Frustration, dejection, bloodshed, vengeance, disease, deformity, blindness—instead of hesitating, one faces them because hidden beneath are rare grains of truth! One would not perish if one confronted them! 'Let the world perish, not I!'

But no, why should the world perish either? Since I have shared its sufferings, how can the truth I have discovered be mine alone? A time comes when the superficial distinction between the 'self' and the 'others' is erased. They are no longer separate.

This is the 'whole' truth. I have 'personally' discovered it—but its dignity lies in its being widely shared once again.

DHARAMVIR BHARATI

A Note to the Directors

I have tried to find answers to the problems raised in this verse play (*drishya kavya*) by seeking help from the last half of the Mahabharata. The main plot of the story is well-known; only a few events have been invented—a few characters and a few incidents. Classical aesthetic theories sanction such interpolations. The two guards, who comment on the events throughout, are a bit like the ordinary citizens who form the chorus in Greek plays; but they are also important symbolic figures. According to the *Bhagavata Purana*, the name of the man who killed Lord Krishna is 'Jara', but I have imagined him as the incarnation of the Old Mendicant.

The entire plot is divided into five acts with an 'Interlude'. There can be an interval after the 'Interlude'. The stage design is not complicated: there is a permanent curtain at the back, and two more curtains in addition. The proscenium curtain is raised at the beginning of each act and is not dropped till the end of the act. Scene changes in the course of each act are indicated by the lifting or dropping of the curtain in the middle of the stage. The curtains in the middle and at the back are not to be painted. The stage must be as bare as possible. Lighting should be restrained but imaginative.

The choric songs are arranged between the acts in a style borrowed from the traditions of Indian folk theatre. The chorus is either used to give information about events which are not shown on stage or to underline the poignancy of the action. Sometimes, it also clarifies the symbolic importance of the events. There should be two choric voices—of a woman and a man and the choric verses should be divided between them, especially when the rhythm or tone changes. Instrumental music accompanying the chorus should be kept at the minimum.

The dialogue is written in free verse. The 'Interlude' has sections which are written in poetic prose, which has also been used elsewhere in the play. In a long play it is important to change the rhythm to avoid monotony. The exception is the dialogue between the two guards, which has the same rhythm from beginning to end. It is not necessary, however, for the speeches of the other characters to follow a specific rhythm and meter. A character should adopt the rhythms which would express his changing emotions and feelings. A lyric may require a consistency of rhythm and tone, which a play may not. Indeed, there are times when there is a rapid change in tone and rhythm in keeping with changing feelings. This is specially so in the case of Sanjaya, where the changes are sudden.

When *Andha Yug* was first presented, the actors faced a peculiar difficulty. They either read their dialogues as if they were written as rhythmic poetry or read them as prose pieces. The solution lies somewhere in the middle. The emphasis should be on conveying the meaning rather than on meter, but the poetic rhythms should also be heard. It is true that this play represents the beginning of the tradition of verse plays, but the recent radio production of *Andha Yug* by Shree Gopal Das succeeded in obtaining a harmony among poetic rhythm, dramatic narrative, and meaning; indeed, its use of volume, undertones, overtones, overlapping tones and tenor etc. revealed the boundless possibilities, not only for the performance of this play, but also for the entire range of new poetry.

Basically, this verse play is designed for the stage. The published text has kept that in mind. The radio production not only helped its cast, but also helped me in polishing its language. The published text has also kept in mind the structures of folk-plays so that it can be adapted for open-air performances. Imaginative directors can also create symbolic stage designs.

DHARAMVIR BHARATI

Characters

ASHWATTHAMA
GANDHARI
DHRITARASHTRA
KRITAVARMA
SANJAYA
OLD MENDICANT
GUARD 1
GUARD 2
VYASA
VIDURA
YUDHISHTHIRA
KRIPACHARYA
YUYUTSU
DUMB SOLDIER
BALARAMA
KRISHNA

The Time of Action

The play begins on the evening of the eighteenth day of the war and ends with the final pilgrimage and death of Lord Krishna.

Prologue

INVOCATION

Narayanam namaskritya naram chaiv narrottamam
daveem sarasawteem vaysaam tato jayamudeeyaret.

PROCLAMATION

This play is concerned
with the age of darkness
which in the *Vishnu Purana*
is described thus:

'*Tataschanudinamalpala haras*
vavachchhedada-dharama-arth-ayorjagatas-samakshayo bhavishyati.'

> ... And then in the future
> day by day
> there will be a decline
> in prosperity and dharma
> and the whole earth shall slowly perish.

'*Tatascharth evabhijan hetu.*'

> The one who has wealth
> shall rule.

'*Kapatavesha dharanameva mahatva hetu.*'

> The one who wears
> a false mask
> shall be honoured.

'*Evam chati lubdhak raja*
sahaas-shailanam-antaradroneeh praja samsriyashyanti.'

> The one who is greedy
> shall be king.

And weary of misrule
the people
shall hide in dark caves
and wait
for their days of misery
to end.

Hide
in real caves
or in the caverns of their souls.

(*A dancer performs as if he is trying to hide in a dark cave and then makes his
exit.*)

In those dark ages
which came into being
at the end of the great war
all thoughts and deeds of men
were corrupt and perverse.

Yes, there were still frail threads
of honour which held men together
but good and evil were so intricately knotted
that only Krishna had the courage to unravel them.

Krishna alone was dispassionate and detached.
Krishna alone
could be the saviour
of their future.

All the others were blind
self-absorbed
depressed and confused
lost in the dark caverns
of their souls.

This is the story of the blind—
or of enlightenment
through the life of the blind.

ACT ONE

The Kaurava Kingdom

(The trumpet blows thrice.)

THE NARRATOR: Both sides in the war
violated
the code of honour
smashed it
ripped it into shreds
and scattered it—
the Kauravas perhaps more than the Pandavas.

When will this bloodshed end?

    This is a strange war
    in which both sides
    are doomed to fail.

    Blindness rules this age
    not reason
    and blindness shall prevail
    in the end.

    Blind fear and blind love
    blind power and blind justice
    shall prevail in the end.

Whatever is good and gentle and beautiful
shall be defeated in the end—
and thus the *dwapara yug* shall pass.

(The curtain rises.)

This is the last evening of the great war.

A profound sadness lies over everything.

In the desolate corridors of this palace
　　of the Kauravas
two old guards pace up and down
up and down.

(*The stage is empty. Two guards enter from the left and the right. They carry spears and shields and pace up and down the stage.*)

GUARD 1:　　　　We are tired
very tired.
Yet we march up and down
guarding these desolate corridors.

GUARD 2:　　　　In these desolate corridors
richly inlaid with jewels
Kaurava queens
once wandered gracefully
like the fragrant breeze.

Today
they are widows.

GUARD 1:　　　　We are tired
very tired.

We are not warriors.
We have shown no courage.
We have not fought
in this grim war
that lasted
seventeen days.

These our spears
these our shields
lie unused
a burden
on our shoulders.

We are just guards
but there is nothing
here to defend.

GUARD 2:   There is nothing here
             to defend.

             This is the kingdom
             of an old and blind ruler
             whose children
             in their blindness
             declared a bitter war.

             They thought honour
             was a rotten whore
             who had infected everyone.

             For seventeen days
             we have defended
             the honour
             of a blind
             and sick kingdom.

GUARD 1:   And now
             we are tired
             very tired.

             All our actions
             are meaningless.
             Our faith
             our decisions
             our courage
             our lives
             are meaningless
             utterly meaningless ...

GUARD 2:   Meaningless
             utterly meaningless ...

             And now
             weary of defending
             this meaningless life—
             these desolate corridors—
             we are tired
             very tired.

(They fall silent and begin to pace up and down. The lights suddenly grow dim. The sound of an approaching storm is heard. One guard strains his ears to listen. The other shades his eyes and looks at the sky.)

GUARD 1:   Did you hear
that terrifying
sound?

GUARD 2:   Why has it suddenly
become so dark?
Can you
see anything?

GUARD 1:   How far can the subjects
of a blind king see?

I can't see a thing.
Perhaps, it's a thunderstorm.

(Frightened, the second guard moves up close to him.)

GUARD 2:   No, it's not a thunderstorm!

Look, there are thousands and thousands
of vultures
with their wings
outspread!

(The sound of flapping wings becomes louder as the stage grows darker.)

GUARD 1:   The sky above the city
of the Kauravas
is overcast with vultures!

GUARD 2:   Hide
hide
take cover
under your shield!
The vultures are ravenous!
They feed on the dead!

(*The stage suddenly brightens.*)

GUARD 1:   Look, they are flying
       towards Kurukshetra.

(*The sound of beating wings grows fainter.*)

GUARD 2:   Death has flown over us.

GUARD 1:   A bad omen
       a dreadful omen.
       Who knows
       what will happen
       to the city
       tomorrow?

(*Vidura enters from the left.*)

GUARD 1:   Who goes there?

VIDURA: It is I
       Vidura.
       Did Dhritarashtra
       see that terrifying sight?

GUARD 1:   How could he?
       He is blind.
       Has he ever
       been able
       to see
       anything
       thus far?

VIDURA: I must meet him.
       All the omens are bad.
       Who knows what news
       Sanjaya will bring today?

(*The guards leave. Vidura stands deep in thought.*)

CHORUS:
Is there still no news from Kurukshetra?
Has the ragged Kaurava army won or lost?

That cloud of hungry vultures will soon
descend upon the corpses and devour them.

In the deathly silence of the court
Gandhari—pale with anxiety—
sits with her head bowed.

Dhritarashtra waits in silence
for Sanjaya to bring him news.

(The curtain rises to reveal an inner room of the palace. Gandhari is seated on a low stool covered by a mat. Dhritarashtra is seated on a small throne. Vidura walks up to them.)

DHRITARASHTRA:
Is that you, Sanjaya?

VIDURA:
No.
It is Vidura, Maharaj.

The whole city
is worried today.

The few who have
survived—ten or twenty—
are waiting
anxiously
for Sanjaya to arrive.

(Waits for Dhritarashtra to say something.)

Maharaj
why don't you
say something?
Even Gandhari
is silent?

DHRITARASHTRA:
Vidura
for the first time

in my life
I am afraid.

VIDURA: Afraid?
The fear you experience today
had gripped others years ago.

DHRITARASHTRA: Why didn't you warn me then?

VIDURA: Bhishma did.
So did Dronacharya.
Indeed, in this very court
Krishna advised you:
'Do not violate the code of honour.
If you violate the code of honour
it will coil around the Kaurava clan
like a wounded python
and crush it like a dry twig.'

DHRITARASHTRA: Vidura
try to understand.
I was born blind.
How could I have discerned the real world
or recognized its social codes?

VIDURA: You could have.
Just as you
accepted the world
in spite of your blindness.

DHRITARASHTRA: But I had created that world
out of the darkest recesses of my own being.

My senses were limited by my blindness.
They defined
the boundary of my material world.

I had spun an illusory world
of dreams and desires and passions
out of the depths of that darkness.

My love, my hate, my law, my dharma
had evolved out of my peculiar world.

My ethics had no other frame of reference.

My sons were the flesh of my flesh
they were the final arbiters of truth for me.
My love for them was my law
my code of honour.

VIDURA: Yet from the very first day
it was obvious that the Kaurava might
—the final arbiter of truth—
was weak and vulnerable.

Over the past seventeen days
you have received news
of the death
—one by one—
of the entire Kaurava clan.

DHRITARASHTRA: The news did not mean much to me.

I was born blind.

All I can do is listen.

Sanjaya describes the world in words
but I still can't visualize anything—
can't see the events his words create.

I can't picture how blood spurted
from Dushasana's shattered chest—
how cruel Bhima collected it
in his cupped hands
and raised them to his lips.

GANDHARI: (*Covering her ears*)

Maharaj

                          don't repeat that!
                          I can't bear it.
(*Everyone falls silent.*)

DHRITARASHTRA: Today
                          I realized
                          that there is a truth
                          that lies beyond the boundaries
                          of my selfhood.
                          I realized that only today.

                          I feel as if a dam has suddenly burst
                          and the violent sea
                          with its poison-tongued waves
                          has crashed through the defences
                          of my narrow well-bounded world
                          filled every corner of my being
                          with its deafening roar
                          and swept away everything—
                          all my personal beliefs
                          my blind faith.

VIDURA: Knowledge acquired
                          through suffering
                          and defeat
                          will give you courage
                          to endure suffering.

DHRITARASHTRA: No, Vidura.

                          What I have
                          learnt today
                          terrifies me.
                          For the first time
                          in my life
                          I am afraid.

VIDURA: Where there is fear
                          there is imperfect knowledge.

As Krishna said:
    'In order to know
    the truth
    surrender your
    heart and mind
    to me.
    Released from fear
    you will
    find me.
    You must have faith.'

GANDHARI: (*Agitated*)

    I don't have faith!
    Perhaps others do.
    I don't.

    'Surrender your
    heart and mind
    to me!'

    Did he
    who lost his head completely
    when he was struck
    by Pitama's arrows
    say that?

    Did he
    who violated
    the code of honour
    over and over again
    say that?

DHRITARASHTRA: Calm down, Gandhari
    calm down.
    Do not blame anyone.

    I was blind …

GANDHARI: But I was not blind.

I had seen the ways of the world
and knew
that dharma
duty and honour
were illusions.

When the time of reckoning arrives
wisdom and honour
are always useless.

There is a dark abyss in each of us
where a ferocious beast
—a blind beast
who is the master
of all we know and do—
resides and has his home.

Morality, honour, selflessness
and surrender to Krishna
are mere disguises
—masks that cover our blindness.
They are like sightless eyes cut out of rags
and stitched on the faces of puppets.

That is why
sick of all this hypocrisy
I chose to live
with my eyes blindfolded.

VIDURA: You have become cynical
             Gandhari!
             Grief over the death
             of your sons
             has embittered you!
             Didn't you tell
             Duryodhana ...

GANDHARI: I told Duryodhana
                 'O Fool, where there is dharma
                 there is victory.'

There was no dharma on either side.
Each was inspired by blind self-interest.

And the one you call Lord
changed the code of honour
to suit his own ends.

He is a fraud!

DHRITARASHTRA:　Calm down, Gandhari.

VIDURA:　This is the bitter voice
　　　　　of despair.

　　　　　Forgive her, O Lord!
　　　　　Accept her bitter lack of faith
　　　　　as an offering!

　　　　　If you receive only those who have faith
　　　　　who will bless those
　　　　　who have none?

　　　　　Forgive her, O Lord!
　　　　　Grief over the death
　　　　　of her sons
　　　　　has made this mother
　　　　　bitter!

GANDHARI:　Do not call me mother!
　　　　　Even the one you call your Lord
　　　　　calls me mother—
　　　　　a word that pierces
　　　　　my soul like a red-hot iron.

　　　　　Over the last seventeen days
　　　　　all my sons have been killed
　　　　　one by one.

　　　　　With my own hands
　　　　　I removed the bangles

                          on the wrists
                          of their wives
                          and wiped the lines of *sindhur*
                          with the end of my garment.

VOICES OFF-STAGE: Victory to Duryodhana!
                          Victory to Gandhari!
                          May Dhritarashtra
                          the ruler of men
                          be blessed!

DHRITARASHTRA: Go, Vidura
                          see if Sanjaya has returned.

GANDHARI: He has won!
                          My son, Duryodhana, has won!
                          Didn't I tell you
                          he would certainly be
                          victorious today?

(A guard enters.)

GUARD: A mendicant, Maharaj
                          an old mendicant.

(An old mendicant enters.)

VIDURA: A mendicant
                          with a broad forehead
                          white hair
                          long limbs?

MENDICANT: I am that future
                          which today
                          in this city of the Kauravas
                          has proved to be false.

                          I used to chart the paths of stars
                          calculate their speed, map their positions
                          read the destiny of men
                          in the unwritten book of fate.

I am an astrologer
from a distant land.

DHRITARASHTRA: I think I remember you.
You had said:
'War is inevitable
and the Kauravas shall be victorious.'

MENDICANT: Yes, I am that man.

Today, all my knowledge
has proved to be false.

Suddenly, a man intervened.
He was stronger and swifter than
the changing constellations.

When Arjuna stood
despondent in the battlefield
He said to him:
'I am omniscient.
Do what I tell you.
Truth shall prevail.
I am the truth.
Do not be afraid.'

VIDURA: He is the Lord!

GANDHARI: No! Impossible!

VIDURA: He is the beginning
and the end of all history.
He determines the course
of all the celestial stars.

MENDICANT: I did not know then
that he was the Lord.

But that day
I suddenly understood

as if in a flash of revelation
that when a man
surrenders his selfhood
and challenges history
he can change the course
of the stars.

The lines of fate
are not carved in stone.
They can be drawn and redrawn
at every moment of time
by the will of man.

GANDHARI: Guard, give him a handful of coins.

(*The guard leaves.*)

You had said:
    'Duryodhana shall be victorious!'

MENDICANT: I am a false prophet and
at this moment my words
have no value.

Many false prophecies
broken dreams
half truths
lie scattered
in every nook and corner
of the city of the Kauravas.

It is unfortunate that Gandhari
fondly nurtures each one of them.

(*The guard returns with a bag of coins.*)

Victory to Duryodhana!
Victory to Gandhari!

(*The mendicant leaves.*)

GANDHARI: Victory shall be ours.
                       I am confident.
                       Victory shall be ours.

                       My hopes may be false
                       or blind
                       but Duryodhana
                       shall be victorious.

                       He shall be victorious!

(*A guard enters and lights the lamps.*)

VIDURA: The sun has set.

DHRITARASHTRA: But
                       Sanjaya has not yet returned.

                       All the soldiers
                       must have gone back
                       to their camps.

                       I want to know—
                       who won
                       who lost?

VIDURA: Maharaj!
                       Do not despair.
                       Sanjaya shall bring you good news.

                       Gandhari, go and rest now.

                       The city gates, like vigilant eyes
                       Are open, and wait
                       For Sanjaya's chariot to arrive.

(*Vidura exits from one side and Dhritarashtra and Gandhari exit from the other. The two guards once again begin to march across the stage.*)

GUARD 1:   Honour!

GUARD 2:	Disbelief!
GUARD 1:	Sorrow at the death of one's sons!
GUARD 2:	The future that is waiting to be born!
GUARD 1:	All these grace the lives of kings!
GUARD 2:	And the one they worship as their Lord takes responsibility for all of them!
GUARD 1:	But what about the lives the two of us have spent in these desolate corridors?
GUARD 2:	Who shall take responsibility for us?
GUARD 1:	We did not violate honour because we did not have any.
GUARD 2:	We were never tormented by disbelief because we never had any faith.
GUARD 1:	We never experienced any sorrow.
GUARD 2:	Nor felt any pain.
GUARD 1:	We spent our desolate lives in these desolate corridors.
GUARD 2:	Because we were only slaves.
GUARD 1:	We merely followed the orders of a blind king.
GUARD 2:	We had no opinions of our own. We made no choices.
GUARD 1:	That is why

from the beginning
we have paced these desolate corridors
from right to left
and then from left to right
without any meaning
without any purpose.

GUARD 2:   Even after death
we shall pace
the desolate corridors
of death's kingdom
from right to left
and then from left to right.

(*They continue to pace up and down. The stage slowly grows dark.*)

CHORUS: Under the shadow of defeat
this city has slowly lost its sense of honour.

Under the shadow of defeat and fear and doubt
false hope hobbles down the desolate streets
like a shrivelled old beggar
pleading with his hands outstretched
for some charity, for some mercy.

There are still two fading embers left in the ruined
    city.
A blind and self-deceiving king
shuffling in the void of his own circle of darkness
and a bewildered
heart-broken Gandhari
still clinging to hope with blind desperation.

And the prophetic Sanjaya
—immortal and detached—
who sees all and knows all
who fears not the wars that Gods promote
who is free from doubts and confusions
who can dare to confront the king with the truth—

even that Sanjaya
is ensnared by the dark night of delusions
and stands lost
on this path of thorns and stones.

ACT TWO

The Making of a Beast

CHORUS: Even Sanjaya
—that rational sculptor of words—
is bewildered in this forest
of doubt and confusion.

His responsibility is great
his words are few
his listeners are blind.

But at this moment of danger
only he can tell the truth.

And yet even Sanjaya
— ensnared by this night of delusions—
stands distracted
on this path of thorns and stones.

(The curtain rises. We see a path through a forest. A soldier, who has laid his weapons aside, lies on the ground with his face covered. Sanjaya enters.)

SANJAYA: I have lost my way
on this path of thorns and stones.
How far is Hastinapur?
Will I ever reach it?

What will I tell them?

There is no dearth of words
but what shall I tell them?

O, why am I still alive
after this shameful defeat?

How shall I tell them?

Even today
there is no dearth of words.

I used to carry
the news of the war to them
describe each event as it happened.

But today
the experience of our final defeat
has changed the very nature of truth.

And today
how shall I use the same words
to carry the burden
of this defeat?

(*The soldier suddenly wakes up and calls, 'Sanjaya'.*)

Who called me?
Was it a ghost
or the voice of my own fears?

KRITAVARMA: Don't be afraid.
It's me, Kritavarma.

So, you are still alive, Sanjaya?
Did the Pandava soldiers
let you go?

SANJAYA: Yes, I am still alive.
The earth for miles around is strewn
with the corpses of Kaurava soldiers
slaughtered by Arjuna.
The Kaurava army is scattered;
all its heroes are dead.

Only I am alive.

When Satyaki raised his sword
to strike me down

—oh, how I wish he had killed me—
Vyasa told him:
    'Sanjaya cannot die.
    He is immortal.'

Unwittingly
Vyasa cursed me:
    'You will survive
    disasters, floods, revolutions,
    and wars of annihilation
    so that you can tell the truth.'

But
how can I tell
the truth to the blind?

It was an utterly new experience
to feel the cold edge of Satyaki's sword
and know that death was so close.

It was a moment of supreme terror.
I felt as if someone had slashed
through all the experiences of my soul
as swiftly as an arrow
slices through a lotus stem.

How can I
after my humiliating experience
tell them the whole truth?

KRITAVARMA: Be brave, Sanjaya,
    for only you can
    tell them
    about Duryodhana's defeat.

SANJAYA: What shall I tell them?

    That the bravest of warriors
    stood next to his shattered chariot

>　　barefoot
>　　disarmed
>　　bloodstained
>　　defeated?
>
>　　That
>　　when he saw me
>　　he lowered his head
>　　and cried?
>
>　　How shall I tell them?
>　　How shall I tell them that?

(*Exit Sanjaya.*)

KRITAVARMA:　Even Sanjaya has left.

>　　Many days ago
>　　Vidura had prophesied
>　　defeat.
>
>　　Today we are defeated.

(*Someone calls from off-stage: 'Ashwatthama'. Kritavarma listens. Kripacharya enters.*)

>　　That sounded like the voice
>　　of old Kripacharya.

(*The call is repeated, 'Ashwatthama …'*)

KRIPACHARYA:　Yes, I am alive.
　　　　　　　　Did Ashwatthama escape?

KRITAVARMA:　Yes.
　　　　　　　　Only three of us
　　　　　　　　are alive today.

>　　When Duryodhana
>　　got off his chariot

and bowed his head in defeat
Ashwatthama saw him.

He turned away
smashed his bow
in despair
and disappeared
into the forest.

(They both exit, calling out to Ashwatthama. Their voices grow fainter. Darkness.
Then light falls on Ashwatthama, who sits with his broken bow in his hand.)

ASHWATTHAMA: This is my bow
the bow of Ashwatthama
which Duryodhana himself
had strung.

Today
I smashed it
in despair
when I saw him
disarmed and helpless
with tears in his eyes.

My bow
is a crushed snake
terrified
and helpless
like my mind.

How shall I
now gather courage
to avenge
my father's
heartless murder?

In this forest
even in this fearful forest
I cannot forget
how Guru Dronacharya

threw his weapons down
on the battlefield
when he heard Yudhishthira
announce triumphantly:
    'Ashwattahma is dead!'

He had so much faith
in Yudhishthira's truthfulness.

Seeing him unarmed
that cowardly sinner
Dhristadyumna
cut him to pieces
with his sword.

I can never forget that.

My father was invincible.

Yudhishthira's half-truth
killed him.

That day
Yudhishthira's half-truth
ruthlessly slaughtered
all that was good
or gentle
in me.

Honoured as Dharmaraj
he added:
    'The man or the beast.'

Since he could not
distinguish between
man and beast
I decided to turn myself
into a blind, ruthless beast.

But even today

I am lost
in a dark cave—
the blind cave
of defeat.

Listen, Duryodhana!
Listen, Dronacharya!
   I, Ashwatthama
   your, Ashwatthama
—foul as the spittle
stale as the phlegm
left in the mouth
of a dying man—
I, Ashwatthama
am the only one
alive today.

(*Thumps his breast triumphantly.*)

Should I commit suicide?
At least I shall be released
From this impotent existence.

Even if I were to burn
in the fires of hell
I would not
have to endure
so much torment.

(*Someone from the wings calls, 'Ashwatthama'.*)

But no
I shall live
like a blind and ruthless beast
and may
Dharmaraj's prophecy come true!

Let both my hands
turn into claws!
Let these eyes

sharp like the teeth of a carnivore
tear the body
of anyone they see!

From now on
my only dharma is:
    'Kill, kill, kill
    and kill again!'

Let that be
the final purpose
of my existence!

(*He hears footsteps.*)

Someone is coming this way.
Maybe it's a Pandava soldier.

He is alone and unarmed.

I shall hide
take him by surprise and
break his neck with these
hungry claws
as I broke my bow.

(*He hides. Sanjaya enters.*)

SANJAYA: I must go on living.
                   I must.
                   I must go on living.

                   Truth, I know, is bitter.
                   Yet I must tell the truth
                   even the bitterest of truths.

                   I must tell the truth.
                   I must tell the truth
                   and nothing but the truth.
                   That is the ultimate meaning
                   of my ... Ah!

(Ashwatthama attacks him from behind and tries to strangle him.)

ASHWATTHAMA: With these
hungry claws
I shall strangle Yudhishthira
who cried,
'Ashwatthama is dead'.

(Kritavarma and Kripacharya enter.)

KRITAVARMA: *(Screams)*

Let go, Ashwatthama!
It's Sanjaya
not a Pandava.

ASHWATTHAMA: Only kill
and kill, and kill …

KRIPACHARYA: Kritavarma, hold him down.
Hold him down.
What kind of soldier are you
Ashwatthama?

Kill an enemy instead.

Sanjaya cannot be killed.
He took no
sides in the war.
He was neutral.

ASHWATTHAMA: Neutral?
The word neutral
is meaningless.

I am no soldier.
I am a beast
a wild and ferocious beast.

Whoever is not with me
is against me!

KRITAVARMA: You are insane.

               Sanjaya,
               you must leave at once.

SANJAYA: No, do not spare me,
               I beg you.

               Kill me, Ashwatthama
               release me
               from the torment
               of telling the truth
               to the blind.

               It is better to be killed
               than to suffer
               this anguish.

               Kill me, Ashwatthama
               and release me from
               this torture.

(Ashwatthama looks helplessly at Kripacharya and rests his head on Kripacharya's shoulder.)

ASHWATTHAMA: What should I do?

               I don't think
               it is a sin to kill.
               I am now
               obsessed with killing.

               I long to break the neck
               of anyone I meet.

               Tell me what I should do.
               Tell me.

KRIPACHARYA: Calm down, calm down!
               There is …

KRITAVARMA: There is a lot to be done.
Duryodhana is still alive.
Let us go and look for him.

KRIPACHARYA: Sanjaya
do you know
where he is?

SANJAYA: (*In a whisper.*)

Yes.
With his extraordinary powers
he has stilled the waters of a lake.
And there
unknown to the Pandavas
he sits strangely still
on the floor
of that enchanted lake.

KRIPACHARAYA: Bless you, Ashwatthama.

Guide us to that lake, Sanjaya.
Let us find out
what he wants us
to do.

KRITAVARMA: Who is that
old man
coming this way?

KRIPACHARYA: Let us go
before someone
sees us.

ASHWATTHAMA: (*As he leaves.*)

I feel helpless
I have broken my vow.

(*They leave. The stage is empty for a while. The old mendicant enters.*)

MENDICANT: I have wandered far
                  from Hastinapur
                  very far.

                  I am old
                  and cannot see clearly
                  but I thought
                  I saw some people here
                  a moment ago.

                  I wonder if I still
                  have the coins
                  Gandhari gave me
                  when I predicted:
                      'This is inevitable
                      that is inevitable
                      and this will come to pass
                      and that will come to pass.'

                  But today
                  this hour of defeat
                  has only proved
                  how unpredictable
                  the future is.

                  Truth resides
                  in the acts
                  we perform.
                  What man does
                  at each moment
                  becomes his future
                  for ages and ages.

(*He sighs.*)

                  That is why
                  Krishna said to Arjuna:
                      'Lift up your bow, Arjuna.
                      Fight without fear.

The meaning of a man's existence
lies in the actions he performs,
not in his refusal to act.'

(*He sees a broken bow lying on the ground. He bends down to pick it up.*)

Who left his bow here?
Has some other Arjuna
begun to doubt?

(*Ashwatthama enters.*)

ASHWATTHAMA: That bow
is mine.

MENDICANT: Who are you?
Victory to Ashwatthama!

ASHWATTHAMA: Victory?
Do not mock me, old man.
This bow was as useless
as your knowledge
of astrology.

I just saw Duryodhana
whose head
was once adorned
by a crown of jewels.

Today, that head
lies covered
by a shroud
of dirty water.

You had prophesied,
'Duryodhana shall be victorious.'

MENDICANT: But Duryodhana shall be victorious!
I still predict that.
I am old

and tired
but I still prophesy:
    'Duryodhana shall never
    be defeated.'

This will be the truth
of the age
about to be born.

The future
I had once prophesied
turned out to be false.

Now I shall go and tell Duryodhana:
    'The future is never independent
    of the present moment.'

There is still time, Duryodhana
there is still time.
Each moment
can transform
history and time.

(*He walks towards the exit slowly.*)

ASHWATTHAMA: What should I do now?
What should I do?

I am trapped in present time
and condemned
to seek vengeance!
Yudhishthira's half-truth
has murdered my future.

And yet
I shall live.

If my damnation
has been already foretold
then nothing matters.

If the future
is indifferent
it is my enemy.

(*He follows the old mendicant.*)

You are a false prophet!
You are an old fraud!

Today
you shall not escape
these hungry claws.

Stop, stop
you old fraud!

(*Gnashing his teeth, he runs after the old mendicant, grabs him by his neck and drags him off stage.*)

Kill, kill, kill.
It is my dharma
to kill.

(*Sounds of a man being strangled as Ashwatthama laughs hysterically. Silence. The stage turns dark. Then a spot of light indicates Sanjaya. Kripacharya, and Kritavarma drag Ashwatthama away from the old mendicant.*)

KRIPACHARYA: What have you done
Ashwatthama?
What have you done?

ASHWATTHAMA: I do not know
what I have done.
Have I done something?

KRITAVARMA: There is something
terrifying
about Ashwatthama.

(*Kripacharya forces Ashwatthama to sit down, loosens his cummerbund and wipes his forehead.*)

KRIPACHARYA: Sit down.
                 Relax.
                 You have done nothing.
                 It was only a terrifying
                 nightmare.

ASHWATTHAMA: What should I do?
                 I don't think
                 it is a sin to kill.
                 I am now
                 obsessed with killing.

                 As I struggled with him
                 I felt strangely calm.
                 I was no longer
                 a snarling beast.
                 I felt utterly detached.

KRIPACHARYA: (*Persuades Ashwatthama to lie down.*)

                 Close your eyes for a while.
                 Sleep.
                 Duryodhana has ordered us
                 to rest today.
                 We shall see
                 what the Pandavas
                 do tomorrow
                 and then decide.

                 Come, turn over
                 and rest for some time.

(*To Kritavarma*)

                 He is asleep.

KRITAVARMA: (*Mockingly*)

                 Asleep!
                 We call ourselves soldiers!

Did we survive
this war
so that
we could hide
in ambush
and kill
old and unarmed men?

KRIPACHARYA: Calm down.
Have you forgetten
the heroic deeds
of the brave warriors
in this war?

Drona was old
and unarmed
but did
Dhristadyumna
spare his life?

Did we
take pity
on Abhimanyu
when he was alone
and trapped
by seven valiant heroes?

ASHWATTHAMA: I did not kill him!
I was blind with rage.
I wanted to annihilate
the future which has been
prophesied.

Believe me
I do not know how
the old man was killed.

KRIPACHARYA: Go to sleep now.
You too, Kritavarma.
I shall keep watch
through the night.

(*He begins to pace up and down.*)

CHORUS:

Like the flood waters of the Ganga
—which sweep the shores and recede
leaving behind disfigured corpses—
the swift and changing tides of history
have swept Ashwatthama away and flung him
on the endless shores of desolate time.

This is a night of lost souls
this is a night of despairing souls
this is a night of shattered souls.

This is a night of intoxication
for the victorious Pandavas.
This is a night of concealment
for the defeated Duryodhana.

This is a night of pride
when heads are held high.
This is a night of shame
when hands lie paralysed.

ACT THREE

The Half-truth of Ashwatthama

THE NARRATOR: When Sanjaya's chariot
reached the city gates
it was dusk.

People asked each other:
   'When will the vanquished
   Kaurava army return?'

They listened
to Sanjaya's account
of the war
till the sun rose again.

His painful story
turned Gandhari
into stone.
Her face
pale with sorrow
seemed lifeless.

As the sun
rose in the sky
the city
slowly stirred
to life.

A rabble
of brahmins
women
doctors
widows
dwarfs
old men
and
the wounded

crawled back
into the city
on broken chariots
and shattered carts.

Eighteen days ago
the soldiers had left
in a riot
of colourful flags
their feet
trampling the earth
their shouts
shattering the sky.

Now
they limp back
in defeat
and disgrace.

(The curtain rises. The guards are on duty. Dhritarashtra enters, leaning on Vidura's shoulder.)

DHRITARASHTRA: I am blind
but with these hands
I felt the wounds
of the soldiers.

Every cut
every stab
seemed like a fatal blow
against my kingdom.

VIDURA: Maharaj
why dwell upon
such thoughts?

DHRITARASHTRA: For no real reason
except that
today I felt
as if those wounds of war

Sanjaya had described so often
had been inflicted on my body.

(*Meanwhile, a soldier, whose tongue has been cut out and who has lost his hearing, crawls onto the stage. He grabs Vidura's feet to draw attention to himself. He cups his hands and begs for water.*)

VIDURA: (*Startled*) What? Oh, no!
Guard, give him some water.

DHRITARASHTRA: Who is it, Vidura?

VIDURA: A thirsty soldier, Maharaj.

(*The soldier makes incomprehensible noises.*)

DHRITARASHTRA: What is he saying?

VIDURA: He says:
'Victory to Dhritarashtra.'

His tongue has been cut out.
He cannot speak.

DHRITARASHTRA: Today
except for the dumb
who will say:
'Victory to Duryodhana'?

(*The guard brings water. The mute soldier begins to gasp for breath.*)

GUARD 1: (*Touching the soldier's forehead.*)

He has a fever.

DHRITARASHTRA: Give him water
and tell him to rest.

(*The soldier crawls to the back of the stage, lies down, and shuts his eyes.*)

Get him
some clothes from Gandhari.

GUARD 1:   Gandhari has not
appeared in public today
to give alms to the poor.

VIDURA: There are no tears
in her eyes today
no sorrow
no anger.
She sits on the steps
still as a statue
carved out of stone.

(*There is commotion in the wings.*)

DHRITARASHTRA: Guard
go and see
what the noise is about.

(*Exit Guard 1.*)

VIDURA: Maharaj
please go and console
Gandhari.

DHRITARASHTRA: I shall.
Even Sanjaya is not with her.
Who knows what news he will
bring today
of the last battle
between Bhima and Duryodhana.

VIDURA: Maharaj
this way.

(*Dhritarashtra leaves with Guard 2.*)

What noise is that?

(*Guard 1 returns.*)

GUARD 2:   Terror
            and panic
            have suddenly
            gripped the city.

VIDURA: Why?

GUARD 1:   An enemy soldier
            a giant of a man
            fully armed
            has slipped into the city
            with our defeated army.
            The people are terrified.
            They think
            he will ransack their homes.

(*Guard 2 returns.*)

VIDURA: Rubbish!
            These are merely rumours.
            Don't believe them.
            I shall go and see for myself.
            Guard the palace
            during my absence.

(*Vidura leaves.*)

GUARD 2:   Did you see the soldier
            with your own eyes?

GUARD 1:   He is a sorcerer
            a shape-changer
            who can take any form
            at will.

            When the guards
            locked the city gates
            he changed into

> a vulture
> flew over
> the locked gates
> and began to prey
> upon the bodies of children
> sleeping on open terraces.

GUARD 2:   Quick!
Lock the western gate
at once.

GUARD 1: (*Terrified*) Look!

GUARD 2:   What is it?

GUARD 1:   He's coming!

GUARD 2:   Quick
take cover, here!

(*Both hide in the shadows at the back. An ordinary-looking soldier enters.*)

YUYUTSU: To be frightened
is not as great
a cause of agony
as to be
the object of fear.

Such is my fate
today.

This is the palace
of my father and mother.
Yet I am apprehensive.
Will they greet me
with a spear
dipped in poison?

GUARD 1:   That is Yuyutsu
Dhritarashtra's son

who fought
on Yudhishthira's side
in the war.

YUYUTSU: What is my crime?
That I was on the side of truth?
No other warrior—
neither Drona nor Bhishma—
dared to oppose Duryodhana.
Only I had the courage
to declare:
          'I will not fight
          on the side of untruth.
          I may be a Kaurava
          but truth is higher
          than my clan!'

GUARD 2:   It is Yuyutsu!
He seems to have returned
with the defeated army.

YUYUTSU: If only
I had turned a blind eye
to Duryodhana's wiles!
My family
would not have
received me
with such cold contempt.
My mother would have
greeted me
with open arms
despite the disgrace
of defeat.

(*Vidura enters.*)

VIDURA: Yuyutsu!
I have been
searching for you
for a long time

my son!
I am glad you have returned.

Guard
go and inform Gandhari
that Yuyutsu is here.

(*Guard 2 leaves.*)

The slaughter of her sons
has left her inconsolable.
Your arrival
may comfort her.

YUYUTSU: I do not know
if she would
even want
to see my face.

VIDURA: Do not say that.
In this evil episode
you are the only one
of the Kaurava clan
who has held his head high
with pride.

YUYUTSU: (*Laughs bitterly*)

That is why
the moment they saw me
the people of the city
shut their doors in fear.

They said:
    'He is a sorcerer
    a giant
    a child-eater
    a vulture!'

VIDURA: Do not pay
too much attention to them
Yuyutsu.

Whenever someone
turns away
from well-worn traditions
and seeks to find
his own path
the ignorant
the cowardly
the simple-minded
always treat him
with contempt.

(*Gandhari enters with a guard. Yuyutsu touches her feet. Gandhari stands still.*)

VIDURA: Gandhari!
This is Yuyutsu.
He is touching your feet.
Give him your blessings.

GANDHARI: (*After a moment's silence.*)

Vidura
ask him
if he is well.

(*Vidura and Yuyutsu remain silent.*)

Son
I hope
those strong arms of yours
are not tired
from slaughtering
your relatives
are they?

(*Silence*)

After the splendour
of the Pandava camp
this city of yours
must seem
drab to you?

(*Silence*)

Why are you silent?

He must be tired, Vidura.
Make a bed of flowers for him.
He is no defeated Duryodhana
who must sleep
on the muddy floor
of some silent lake.

(*Silence*)

Vidura
why is he silent?
Is it because
I am the mother
of his enemies?

(*Turns to leave*)

Guard
let us go back.

VIDURA: Gandhari!
                 This does not become you!

(*Gandhari keeps walking.*)

YUYUTSU: Why did my mother do that
                 Vidura?
                 Why did she do that?

(*He sits with his head in his hands.*)

It would have been better
if I had
accepted
the untruth.

VIDURA: That would have been
no solution
to the problem!
If you had accepted
the untruth
your soul
would have been
scarred irredeemably.

YUYUTSU: As if my mother's curse
and the people's hate
will save me
from damnation!
In the final analysis
whether you uphold truth
or untruth
you are damned.
Vidura
what did I gain?
What did I gain?

VIDURA: Be calm, Yuyutsu.
Endure it all.
Great suffering
must be endured
with grace.

(*The sound of a man gasping for breath, which has been audible for some time, becomes louder.*)

GUARD 1: What noise is that?
Perhaps
that soldier who cannot speak
is nearing his end.

(*The guard fetches water.*)

VIDURA: Give him some water
                     Yuyutsu.
                     Treat him with kindness
                     give comfort to the dying
                     and endure suffering
                     without bitterness.

YUYUTSU: (*Goes up to the soldier.*)

                     Here
                     rest your head
                     in my lap.
                     Come
                     open your mouth.
                     Yes, that's right.
                     Open your eyes
                     and look at me.

(*The soldier opens his eyes, and is about to drink water, when he shrieks.
He crawls away in terror and tries to escape.*)

GUARD 2:   What happened?

YUYUTSU: It is my fault.
                     He was in the cavalry
                     of the Kaurava army.
                     My fire-tipped arrows
                     burnt
                     his knees
                   . to cinders.

                     How can he now
                     accept mercy
                     from one
                     who destroyed his life?

                     I have changed so much
                     that if I now offer love
                     no one will accept it.

Vyasa told me:
'Where there is Krishna
there is victory.'

Yes
Krishna is victorious
but I am damned.
I am
cursed by my mother
reviled as a murderer
and hated by everyone.

VIDURA: Today
in this hour of defeat
I do not know
where righteousness ends
and falsehood begins.

Everyone has lost
his bearings today.
T! ɔ axle is broken
and the wheel spins
without a centre.

Are you there, O Lord?
Are you there?

(*Suddenly, there is a frightening scream off-stage.*)

YUYUTSU: What was that, Vidura?

VIDURA: Guard, go and see.

(*The guard goes out and returns immediately.*)

GUARD 1:   Sanjaya
has brought the news that ...

VIDURA and
YUYUTSU: (*Together.*) What!

GUARD 1:   That ... in the final combat ...
                      Duryodhana ...
                      has been defeated ...

(*Vidura and Yuyutsu rush out. The sound of weeping becomes louder. Someone shouts: 'Duryodhana has been defeated.' The curtain at the back rises. We see Pandava soldiers celebrating their victory. The scene fades. Then, we see a forest path. Kritavarma and Kripacharya rush in carrying bows and arrows.*)

KRITAVARMA: Find somewhere to hide
                      Kripacharya.
                      Elated by their victory
                      the Pandava soldiers
                      are returning
                      to their camp.
                      The air resounds
                      with the sound
                      of conch-shells.

KRIPACHARYA: Wait.
                      Pick up your bow.
                      Someone is coming this way.

KRITAVARMA: Don't shoot!
                      It's Ashwatthama.
                      He had gone in disguise
                      to see the final battle
                      between Duryodhana and Bhima.

(*Ashwatthama enters.*)

ASHWATTHAMA: Duryodhana
                      was killed by treachery.

KRIPACHARYA: (*Signals to him to be silent.*)

                      Hide!
                      Enraged with the Pandavas
                      Balarama is coming this way.

KRITAVARMA: (*Looking towards the wings*)

> Krishna
> is with him.

KRIPACHARYA: Listen
> listen carefully.

BALARAMA: (*From the wings*)

> No!
> No!
> No!
> Say what you like, Krishna
> but what Bhima did today
> violated dharma.
> His attack
> was an act
> of betrayal.

KRIPACHARYA: I wonder what
> Krishna is trying
> to explain.

BALARAMA: (*Still off-stage*)

> The Pandavas are related to us
> but are the Kauravas our enemies?
> I would have confronted Bhima today
> but you stopped me.
> I have known you since childhood.
> You have always been
> an unprincipled rogue!

KRIPACHARYA: (*Puts his bow down.*)

> They are walking away.

BALARAMA: Krishna
> you can do what you like.

You can go to Hastinapur
and console Gandhari.

But let me tell you
that despite your holiness
and your cunning
the Pandavas
who are celebrating
their victory
with conch shells
will also be destroyed
by adharma.

ASHWATTHAMA: (*Repeating the last phrase.*)

By adharma—
they will also be destroyed
by adharma.

KRIPACHARYA:　　　Son
what is troubling you?

ASHWATTHAMA:　　　They will also
be destroyed by adharma.

I have decided.
I have decided
to kill them.
I, Ashwatthama
will kill them
because they are vile.

KRITAVARMA: (*Mockingly*)

Just as you killed
the old mendicant?

ASHWATTHAMA: (*Irritated*)

Yes.
I will not rest

till I have destroyed
the entire Pandava clan.

KRITAVARMA: But Ashwatthama
the Pandavas are not old men.
They are not unarmed.
They are not alone.

This unrighteous war
is over.

But since you are
burning with courage
go spread your adharma
somewhere else.

ASHWATTHAMA: Don't mock me
Kritavarma!
I am ready to do even that.

But since you sympathize with
the Pandavas
I must kill you first.
Come, pick up your sword.

KRIPACHARYA: Ashwatthama
have you gone mad?
Have you no sense of honour left in you?
Put away your sword.

ASHWATTHAMA: Did you hear that, Father?
I am the only one
who seeks revenge.

Dhristadyumna violated dharma
when he killed you.
Bhima violated dharma
when he killed Duryodhana.
Yet I
poor, orphaned Ashwatthama

must alone carry
the burden of honour and dharma.

KRIPACHARYA: Come
sit next to me, son.
We are with you.
We too desire revenge
but not through treachery.
Find some other way.

ASHWATTHAMA: Some other way!
Have the Pandavas left us
any other options?

The Pandava sense of honour
was on display today
when Bhima
violating all the codes of war
threw Duryodhana down
smashed his thighs
broke his arms and his neck.

And then
with his foot on Duryodhana's head
Bhima stood on him with all his weight
and roared like a wild beast!

The veins on Duryodhana's head
swelled and suddenly burst.
He screamed in pain.
His broken legs jerked.
He opened his eyes
and looked at his people.

KRIPACHARYA: Enough Ashwatthama.
Perhaps your way
is now the only one left.

ASHWATTHAMA: Come
let us swear allegiance.

Do not delay.
Duryodhana may still
be alive.

Proclaim me the commander
of the army
in his presence.

I will find a way
to wreak vengeance.

KRIPACHARYA: Let's go.
                 Come, Kritavarma.

KRITAVARMA: No.
                 Leave me out of this.
                 You go.

(*Kripacharya and Ashwatthama leave.*)

KRITAVARMA: Have they left?
                 I am not a coward.
                 I too am pained
                 by Duryodhana's murder.

But what a grotesque spectacle this is!

A defeated Duryodhana
who does not have an unbroken
bone in his body
anointing
a madman as the commander
of an army of two—
old Kripacharya and cowardly Kritavarma!

Such is the plight
of the invincible Kauravas!

Let it be, Kritavarma.
Do not say anything more.

Having chosen to support
Duryodhana
stand by him
till your last breath.

(*Kripacharya enters.*)

Back so soon
Kripacharya?

KRIPACHARYA: I couldn't bear to look
at that terrible sight anymore!

Two grim vultures
were watching Duryodhana
from the hollow of a tree.
Jackals and wolves
circled him
hiding behind one bush
or the other
    waiting
    watching with hungry eyes
        hungry eyes
        and drooling tongues.

KRITAVARMA: (*Sarcastically*)

Then how was Ashwatthama
anointed as the commander?

KRITAVARMA: Duryodhana said:
    'You are a brahmin
    Kripacharya.
    There is no water here.
    Anoint the brave Ashwatthama
    as the commander
    with your own sweat.

I can't lift my arms
to bless him.

My shoulders
are broken.'

I helped him
lift his lifeless arm
to bless Ashwatthama
but instead of blessing him
he screamed in agony.

ASHWATTHAMA: (*Entering*)

But he will live.
He assured me:
'Ashwatthama
till you
bring me news
of your revenge
I shall refuse to die
even if the wild beasts
tear me from limb to limb.'

Did you hear that, Kritavarma?
By tomorrow
my vengeance will be complete.
I shall wreak it alone
even if no one follows me.

KRITAVARMA: (*Yawns*)

I'll follow you—
Senapati.

ASHWATTHAMA: (*In a strange voice*)

Go to sleep
my soldiers.
Tomorrow
Senapati Ashwatthama
will tell you
what to do.

(*Kripacharya and Kritavarma go to sleep. Ashwatthama picks up his bow and keeps watch.*)

> How still the forest is
> only I am awake
> even the shadows
> of the tamarind
> the banyan
> the peepul
> are asleep…

(*Slowly the stage becomes dark. Somewhere in the forest a jackal howls. Other animals take up his cry. The stage is now dark. Only Ashwatthama can still be seen pacing up and down. Suddenly the harsh cawing of a crow is heard. A dancer, dressed in black and wearing the mask of a crow, enters the stage. He spreads his wings and circles the stage twice, kneels, tilts his head to one side and goes to sleep. During this sequence, Ashwatthama is in darkness while the dancer is lit by a bluish light.*

Then an owl hoots. A dancer, in white tights and wearing the mask of an owl, enters from the right. His hands are like the claws of an owl. The moment he sees the crow, he stops. He flaps his wings excitedly and sharpens his claws.

A spotlight shows Ashwatthama watching the dance of war between the crow and the owl. He seems to be mesmerized.

The crow stirs and opens his eyes. He sees the owl and goes back to sleep. The owl watches the crow nervously. Prods him to make sure that he is really asleep. Then he attacks him. Both fight ferociously. The noise and the screams are terrible. For some time, both are in darkness. Then the lights come on. The owl's claws are red with blood. A few crow feathers float across the stage. The owl picks up the feathers and performs in frenzy the tandava dance of death.

The light on Ashwatthama becomes brighter. He breaks out of his trance and begins to laugh loudly. The owl stops dancing and looks at him nervously. The owl throws the black feathers of the crow at Ashwatthama and leaves as fast as he can.

Ashwatthama picks up the feathers and shouts in excitement.)

ASHWATTHAMA: Got it!
       Got it!
       I have got it!

(*The stage is now fully lit. Ashwatthama dances around the stage in great excitement. He holds the blood-covered feathers in his hands. Startled, Kritavarma and Kripacharya wake up. Kripacharya draws his sword.*)

KRIPACHARYA: What have you found?

ASHWATTHAMA: I have found the truth!
       Ashwatthama
       the beast
       has found the truth!

KRITAVARMA: These bloody and tattered feathers!

ASHWATTHAMA: Yes
       bloody and tattered
       like Yudhisthira's
       half-truth!

KRIPACHARYA: Where are you going?

ASHWATTHAMA: To the Pandava camp.
       They must be unarmed and asleep.
       The victorious Pandavas!

(*He fastens his cummerbund.*)

KRIPACHARYA: Now?

ASHWATTHAMA: Now!
       At once!
       They are alone.
       Krishna has gone to Hastinapur
       to console Gandhari.
       When will we get
       a better chance?

KRITAVARMA: Is that the Senapati's order?

ASHWATTHAMA: (*Without having heard Kritavarma.*)

                   Did he say:
                       'The man or the beast …'

                   Like a beast
                   I will crush
                   Dhristadyumna
                   with my feet—
                   like a mad beast
                   trampling on a lotus flower.

                   I will not even spare
                   Uttara
                   who is carrying Abhimanyu's son
                   and the future
                   of the entire Pandava clan
                   in her womb!

KRIPACHARYA: No, no, no
                   I will not let you do that!

ASHWATTHAMA: I will do it!
                   I will do it alone.
                   Even if you do not help me
                       I will do it!
                       I will!

(*Kritavarma follows him with his head bowed.*)

KRIPACHARYA: Stop!
                   Ashwatthama
                   Think for a moment…

(*Ashwatthama leaves without listening to him. Kripacharya follows him, calling 'Ashwatthama … Ashwatthama … Ashwatthama …' His voice slowly fades. The stage is filled with the clatter of three chariot wheels and the thunder of horses.*)

INTERLUDE

Feathers, Wheels, and Bandages

(The old mendicant enters. The stage is lit by a ghostly light which casts a web-like pattern over everything.)

MENDICANT: I am the old mendicant
murdered by Ashwatthama.
I was a false prophet
now I am only a sad spectre.

Life is an eternal river.
Death grabbed my arm
and dragged me to its shore.

Uninvolved
detached
I now stand upon the shore
and realize
that
this age
is a blind ocean
bounded on all sides
by mountains
and caves
and high cliffs.
Terrible storms
thunder down the mountains
and churn the ocean waters
into a raging whirlpool.

Life in this age
is not a smooth-flowing river
but a dark and tormented ocean
that seethes and surges
like a pit of snakes
in which thousands of serpents

blindly twist and turn
coil and uncoil
creep and curl
and crawl over each other.

Similarly a thousand
streams and rivulets
slither and slide
towards the ocean
like blind snakes.

In this age
life is like
a blind and turbulent ocean.

White snake skins
float on the surface of the sea.

White bandages
cover Gandhari's eyes
and bind the wounds of soldiers.

With my visionary powers
I shall stop the flow
of this narrative
and still
the characters in their places
assign them a function
a purpose
so that I can
rip them open
and understand
their inner contradictions.

Here are
the characters
raised by my visionary powers.

They appear
as spectres.

(*Yuyutsu, Vidura, and Sanjaya walk onto the stage as if they are in a trance. They walk mechanically and form a line behind the old mendicant. One by one, they come forward, speak their lines, and fall back in line again.*)

YUYUTSU'S SPECTRE: I am Yuyutsu.

I am like a firm wheel
that was fixed to a chariot
throughout the war.
But now I feel
as if I had spun
on the wrong axle
and have lost my bearings.

SANJAYA'S SPECTRE: I am Sanjaya.

Exiled from the world of action
nailed to the axle
between two great wheels
I am only a small
useless
decorative wheel
which turns
when the great wheels turn
but which neither touches the ground
nor forces the chariot forward.

My greatest misfortune is
that I can never
stop spinning on that axle.

VIDURA'S SPECTRE: I am Vidura
a devout and righteous
follower of Krishna.

In an age where everything is
so strangely complicated
my faith is simple and unassuming.

But now my voice is full of doubt

for it seems that my Lord
is like a useless axle
which has lost its wheels
and cannot turn by itself.

But it is a sin to doubt
and I do not want to sin.

(*There is a sound of bells off-stage. A peacock feather floats across the stage. The old mendicant picks it up.*)

MENDICANT: What is this?
                        A peacock feather?
                        It must have fallen off
                        Krishna's crown
                        when he was returning from Hastinapur
                        after trying to console Gandhari.

(*He stops to listen to the sounds off-stage.*)

                        Yes, they are the bells of his chariot.
                        Should I try to stop him
                        just as I have stopped the flow of this story?

(*He fails to break the spell of Krishna's presence.*)

                        No, I cannot stop him.
                        He is the embodiment of time
                        as it flows in its stately dignity.

(*The sound of another chariot speeding by is heard.*)

                        Yes, there is another chariot
                        which even Krishna cannot stop.
                        It is the chariot of my murderer
                        Ashwatthama.

                        His hatred can never be appeased.
                        It is terrifying like the blood-soaked feather
                        of a black crow!

Can a small peacock feather
defeat it?

Will Krishna be able to squash
this black serpent of hate
which has raised its head once more?

(*The sounds of chariot wheels grow louder.*)

The chariots are speeding away
and I can only watch helplessly.
I can no longer stop
the flow of this story.

Krishna's chariot has been left behind
in the surrounding darkness.

Look!
Ashwatthama's chariot
has reached the Pandava camp!

(*The sounds of chariot wheels stop.*)

But wait
who is that giant-like being
standing in the dark
like a wall of black granite
before Ashwatthama?

(*He covers his eyes in fear. A terrifying roar is heard off-stage. The lights go off and the stage grows dark.*)

ACT FOUR

Gandhari's Curse

CHORUS: It was Shankara
           Ashwatthama saw
terrifying and enormous
       standing before the gate
of the Pandava camp
       threatening annihilation.

It was Shankara
       Ashwatthama saw
thousands of venomous snakes
       encircling his arms
like amulets.

Wrathful
       he stood
before the Pandava camp
       threatening complete annihilation.

'Defeat me
       before you enter!'
He roared in a voice
       more dreadful than thunder.

Ashwatthama attacked him at once
with swords, arrows, spears, and clubs.

Who else
       could have withstood
Ashwatthama's rage
       his superhuman violence?

Shankara's body
       endured
each blow

                        absorbed every thrust
                till Ashwatthama
                    exhausted
                    accepted defeat
                    sank to his knees
                        and begged for
                            mercy.

ASHWATTHAMA'S
VOICE: O Shankara
                        whose braided hair burns wild
                        like flames around cauldron fires
                            bless me!

                    O Shankara
                        whose tresses stream and swirl
                        like storm-entangled whirlpools
                            bless me!

                    O Shankara
                        whose anointed forehead shines and shimmers
                        in the silver light of the new moon
                            bless me!

                    O Shankara
                        whose radiant face glows with splendour
                        and makes every moment of mine a delight
                            bless me!

CHORUS: Easy to please
                    easy to appease
                    Shiva raised his hand
                    and blessed him.

                    'Ashwatthama
                        you will be victorious.

                    The Pandavas have lost
                    their sense of righteousness.

Because I loved Krishna
   I protected them
gave them victory
   renewed their confidence.
But they have violated
   the dharma of war
and opened
   the doors for their destruction.'

Easy to please
easy to appease
Shiva raised his hand
and blessed him.

(*When the curtain rises, we see Gandhari seated. Vidura and Sanjaya, who are standing, seem to be in the middle of a conversation.*)

GANDHARI: What happened next
                Sanjaya?
                Tell me
                what happened after that?

SANJAYA: (*As if repeating a lesson mechanically.*)

                Blessed by Shiva
                that brave warrior
                reached Dhritadyumna's tent
                with the speed of lightning
                dragged him off his bed
                knelt on his chest
                and wrung his neck
                till his eyeballs popped out
                like stones from unripe mangoes
                and blood oozed
                out of the empty sockets.

GANDHARI: He blinded him first!
                That was kind of Ashwatthama!

SANJAYA: Speaking each word with great difficulty

Dhristadyumna pleaded:
   'At least kill me with a sword.'

Aswatthama shouted:
   'No
   you are a coward
   and deserve to die like an animal.
   You killed Drona when he was unarmed.
   This is my revenge.'

Then he kicked him
again and again
till he died.

VIDURA: Enough!
                 Stop it.

GANDHARI: No, go on!
                 What happened next?

SANJAYA: Hearing the commotion
                 The Pandava soldiers woke up.
                 Still rubbing their eyes
                 they staggered out of their tents
                 only to be slaughtered
                 by Ashwatthama's
                 poison-tipped arrows.

                 When Shatanik couldn't find a weapon
                 he picked up a chariot wheel
                 and attacked him.

                 Ashwatthama
                 cut off his legs.

                 Shikhandi was
                 sleeping at a distance.
                 Ashwatthama's arrow split his head in two
                 drilled through the sandalwood cot
                 and buried itself in the ground.

GANDHARI: What happened next?

VIDURA: Your heart is made of stone, Gandhari!

GANDHARI: Diamonds are quarried
              out of stone mines!
              Do not interrupt, Vidura.
              Go on, Sanjaya.

VIDURA: Listen to me
              not to Sanjaya.

              The vengeance
              was terrible.

              Kripacharya and Kritavarma
              waited outside the tents.
              When children, old men, and servants
              ran out in terror
              Kritavarma's arrows
              cut them down.

              Frightened elephants
              trumpeted wildly
              smashed the tents
              and trampled the women
              sleeping inside
              to death.

              And then
              our two heroes
              set the Pandava camp
              on fire.

GANDHARI: I wish I had seen that
              with my own eyes!
              Ashwatthama must have been
              surrounded
              by a halo of light!

SANJAYA: Roaring like a lion
                  Ashwatthama ran
                  like a thing possessed
                  through fire and smoke
                  through blood, guts, and bones
                  wounded horses and broken chariots
                  corpses and severed heads
                  slashed limbs and shattered ribs.

                  Dripping with blood
                  his sword
                  seemed like an extension
                  of his hand.

GANDHARI: Stop, Sanjaya
                  stop.

                  I beg of you!
                  With your visionary powers
                  give me a glimpse
                  of that Ashwatthama!

SANJAYA: It's a horrible sight!
                  He was cruel.
                  He was dreadful.

GANDHARI: But he was heroic!
                  Ashwatthama achieved
                  what a hundred sons of mine
                  could not!
                  What Drona could not!
                  Bhishma could not!

SANJAYA: Vyasa granted me this boon
                  for the limited duration
                  of the war.
                  I do not know
                  when that power
                  will be snatched away from me!

GANDHARI: That is why
I demand it now.

Krishna
who is unjust
will never spare
him after this!

SANJAYA: I shall try.

May the strength
of all my good deeds
in the past
grant you a vision
of Ashwatthama!

(*He concentrates on his prayers.*)

May all the walls disappear
may all the veils of maya be lifted
and the vision be clear!

May the distances vanish
and all that lies beyond
the visible horizon
appear before us!

(*The curtain at the back of the stage lifts and the foreground becomes dark.*)

It is dark.

This is the place
where Duryodhana
lay dying
till yesterday.

Who are those
two armed soldiers?
Kritavarma and Kripacharya?

(*Someone from back-stage calls, 'Maharaj Duryodhana! Maharaj Duryodhana!'*)

KRIPACHARYA: Kritavarma
                    shoot a fire-tipped arrow
                    so we can see in the dark.

KRITAVARMA: (*Looks towards the wings.*)

                    There is Duryodhana.
                    I am sure
                    some wild beast
                    has dragged his half-dead body
                    under that bush.

KRIPACHARYA: He is still alive!
                    He wants to tell us something.

KRITAVARMA: I can't understand
                    what he is trying to say.
                    The blood
                    oozing from his mouth
                    has coagulated
                    and formed a thick black clot
                    around his lips.
                    It must have also choked his throat.

KRIPACHARYA: (*Forming words slowly, he shouts his message to Duryodhana.*)

                    Maharaj
                    Ashwatthama
                    the new general of our army
                    has completely destroyed
                    the Pandava camp.
                    There is not a soldier left alive.

KRITAVARMA: Maharaj's face
                    is glowing
                    with joy.

KRIPACHARYA: His eyes are open!

KRITAVARMA: Whom are they looking for?
               Ashwatthama?

KRIPACHARYA: Maharaj
               Ashwatthama has gone
               to fetch his *Brahmastra*
               and his talisman.
               As soon as he returns
               the three of us
               shall seek refuge
               in the thick forest.

KRITAVARMA: Tears are flowing down his eyes!

(*The light falls on Gandhari and Sanjaya.*)

SANJAYA: Why don't you
               remove the blindfold?

               Look, Ashwatthama is coming
               this way!

GANDHARI: No, no, no!
               I shall not be able to watch
               Duryodhana die.

               Let my eyes remain blindfolded
               Sanjaya.
               Let them be blindfolded.
               But continue to describe
               what is happening there.

VIDURA: I cannot see anything!

SANJAYA: I can see
               Ashwatthama coming this way.
               His head is bowed
               and he is silent.

KRIPACHARYA: Maharaj
               Ashwatthama is here.

Since you cannot
lift your hand
open your eyes
and bless him.

ASHWATTHAMA: No, Maharaj.
No.
I am still not worthy of it.

I have avenged
the sinful murder of my father
by Dhristadyumna.
But I shall have to avenge
your murder.

Yet another task
remains unfinished.

Uttara is still safe.
She will give birth to a son
heir to the Pandava dynasty.

But, Maharaj
I shall complete my task.

When you meet Drona
in the kingdom beyond the sun
tell him…

KRITAVARMA: Whom are you talking to
Ashwatthama?
Maharaj is dead.

(*Mournful music plays in the background. Kripacharya covers his face and falls
to the ground in grief. Gandhari screams and faints.*)

ASHWATTHAMA: Who screamed?

Gandhari
I promise

that just as Krishna destroyed
all the sons
born of your womb
I will destroy
the child
in Uttara's womb.

I will not let that child
be born.

Let Krishna
try to protect him
with his yogic powers.

(*The curtain at the back falls.*)

GANDHARI: Sanjaya
               Sanjaya
               take off my blindfold.
               I want to gaze upon Ashwatthama
               and transform his body
               into a bright diamond.

               There, Sanjaya
               I have taken off this blindfold
               and flung it away.

               Where is Ashwatthama?

SANJAYA: Something strange has happened.
               Suddenly a curtain has fallen
               before my visionary eyes.

GANDHARI: Quick!
               Show me
               before these eyes
               are blinded with tears.

SANJAYA: May these surrounding walls
               vanish!

Let these walls vanish!

Gandhari, Gandhari!
Something has happened
to my visionary power!

Wall!
Walls!
There are walls everywhere!
I cannot open my eyes.

Trying to show the truth
to the blind
must I too become blind?

VIDURA: Sanjaya
       can't you see
       the forest or Duryodhana or ...

SANJAYA: No, Vidura
       only walls
       and walls and more walls!

VIDURA: It is as if
       the time
       for everything to end
       has come.

(*Gandhari sits still.*)

SANJAYA: Vyasa
       why did you
       grant me vision
       for such a short time?

       From today
       I shall never
       be satisfied

by the sight
of this limited world.

My soul shall forever
long to break its limits
and merge with the infinite.

VIDURA: Come, Gandhari.
It is time to leave Hastinapur
and perform
the holy rites for your family.

Sanjaya
inform all our kinsmen
and our dependents
that we shall
leave the battlefield today.

SANJAYA: (*As he leaves*)

For eighteen days
this terrible
but exhilarating war
gave me visionary powers
and then
deprived me of them.

(*Yuyutsu enters.*)

VIDURA: Come, Gandhari.
Let us go.
Call Dhritrashtra.
Yuyutsu
you come with us too.

YUYUTSU: How can these hands
which have shed blood
make ritual offerings
for the dead?

They were my brothers
my kinsmen.

Tell me, Krishna
how can I make
ritual offerings
with these hands?

(Everyone leaves. The stage grows dark. Then the curtain at the back rises.)

CHORUS: They have left.
        The Kaurava city is desolate.
They have left.
        The diamond throne is empty.

They have left.

    The solitary streets
    the city squares
    the homes
    the courtyards
    the gold-domed palaces
    have been taken over
    by wild beasts.

They have left.

The Kaurava city is desolate.

They have left.

    Their widows in chariots
    lead the procession.
    Dhritarashtra, Yuyutsu
    Sanjaya, Vidura, and Gandhari
    slowly shuffle after them.

They have left
    to perform the last rites
    for Gandhari's
    dead sons.

(*Dhritrashtra, Yuyutsu, Vidura, Sanjaya, and Gandhari enter.*)

DHRITARASHTRA: My body is old
and broken.
I cannot walk
any further.

VIDURA: Sanjaya
stop for a moment.

YUYUTSU: Whose chariots are those
beyond the bushes
racing past at such speed?

SANJAYA: The one
over there is Kripacharya's.

VIDURA: And the other
is Kritavarma's.

GANDHARI: Sanjaya
is Ashwatthama there too?

VIDURA: Yes
Ashwatthama is there too.

DHRITARASHTRA: Let him go.

GANDHARI: No, stop him.

SANJAYA: Stop, Ashwatthama
stop!
I am Sanjaya.
Maharaj Dhritarashtra
and Gandhari
are with me
so are Vidura and Yu…

DHRITARASHTRA: Sanjaya
do not utter Yuyutsu's name.

Ashwatthama in his rage
will not spare his life.

How will I live
if I lose him too?

GANDHARI: Especially when the son
                   is Yuyutsu.

                   Hide, Yuyutsu
                   and save your life.
                   Now
                   you are the only protector
                   of your blind father and old mother.

                   Come, Sanjaya
                   let us go.

(*Leaves with Sanjaya.*)

YUYUTSU: I will endure these taunts
                   and live.
                   But for whom?
                   For whom?

DHRITARASHTRA: Son
                   you were conceived in blindness.
                   It defined the boundary of your existence.

                   You tried to escape the enclosing circle
                   and live in a circle of light.

YUYUTSU: Was that a sin?

(*Gandhari and Sanjaya return.*)

DHRITARASHTRA: Have you returned, Sanjaya?

SANJAYA: Ashwatthama
                   is completely transformed.

He is no longer
a brave soldier
but the incarnation of fear.

He trembles so much
that the reins of the chariot
slip out of his hands.

(*The sound of a conch-shell is heard.*)

GANDHARI: He has gone mad.
                     He says
                     he will cover himself
                     with leaves
                     and live in a forest.

                     He is terrified
                     of Krishna.

(*Suddenly, there is an explosion in the distance. A flash of lightning bursts through
the rear of the stage.*)

SANJAYA: Krishna and the Pandavas
                     are coming this way
                     in search of Ashwatthama.

GANDHARI: Krishna will not be able
                     to kill Ashwatthama.

                     For with my glance
                     I had bestowed
                     upon his body
                     the hardness of a diamond.

(*Another explosion is heard in the distance.*)

VIDURA: It seems the Lord
                     has tracked him down.

DHRITARASHTRA: Sanjaya
                     can you see anything?

SANJAYA: Vyasa has taken away
       my visionary powers.

YUYUTSU: The sky is lit
       by Arjuna's fiery arrows.

VIDURA: All the trees and bushes
       have been reduced to ash.

(*Two smouldering arrows fall on the stage.*)

DHRITARASHTRA: Sanjaya
       let us go far away
       from this battlefield.

GANDHARI: Krishna
       if you dare to harm
       Ashwatthama …

(*Smouldering arrows continue to fall on the stage.*)

VIDURA: Let us go, Gandhari.
       It is not safe here.
       Fire-tipped arrows
       are falling all around.

(*They leave. The stage is empty for a few minutes. Then there is the sound of conch-shells mingled with loud explosions. A bright flash of lightning. Suddenly, Ashwatthama comes running on to the stage. An arrow has pierced his neck. He pulls it out. Blood gushes from the wound. Arrows whiz past him. He staggers, but regains his balance. His face glows with anger.*)

ASHWATTHAMA: Arjuna
       defend yourself.

       Defend yourself.

       I wanted to
       cover myself with leaves
       and live in a forest.

But Krishna's
insatiable hunger for war
will not be satisfied
till all the Pandavas
have been killed.

So be it.

Here is the Brahmastra.

> Arjuna
> remember all your
> past deeds.

Not even a hundred million Krishnas
can counter the Brahmastra.

> Listen all you Gods
> in the sky above
> who are watching
> this fight
> you are my witnesses.
> Arjuna has compelled me
> to fight.

> There
> I have released the Brahmastra!

(*He releases the Brahmastra. Lightning, brighter than the sun, flashes across the stage. There is a roar followed by complete darkness.*)

VYASA: (*Speaking from somewhere above*)

> What have you done, Ashwatthama!
> You depraved man!
> What have you done!

ASHWATTHAMA: Who is inviting his own death?

> How dare you stop me
> from seeking revenge!

VYASA: I am Vyasa.

                    O you vile man
                    do you even know
                    the consequences
                    of using the Brahmastra?

                    For centuries to come
                    nothing will grow on earth.
                    Newborn children
                    shall be deformed.

                    Men shall become grotesque.

                    All the wisdom men gathered
                    in the *satya*, *treta*, and *dvapara* yugs
                    shall be lost forever.

                    Serpents shall hiss
                    from every ear of corn
                    and rivers shall flow
                    with molten fire.

ASHWATTHAMA: Let the world
                    be reduced to ash, Vyasa!
                    Let there be a cataclysm!

                    Let me see
                    if Krishna has the power to save it.

VYASA: You are a monster!

                    Even before Krishna could say anything
                    Arjuna released
                    his Brahmastra
                    towards the sky.

                    Soon the two weapons
                    shall collide in the sky.

The sun shall be extinguished.
The earth shall become
a wasteland
of ash and stones!

(*There is a loud explosion. A flash of lightning is followed by complete darkness.*)

ASHWATTHAMA: What could I have done?

Arjuna left me no other choice.

I was alone.

And Krishna
who respects no law
was determined to kill me
with the help of the Pandavas.

(*Terrifying screams can be heard in the distance.*)

VYASA: Listen Arjuna.
I am Vyasa.
Recall your Brahmastra.

Ashwatthama
do not let your cowardice
reduce the earth to a wasteland
of ash and stones.

Recall your Brahmastra
surrender your talismanic gem
and retire into some forest hermitage.

ASHWATTHAMA: Vyasa, I am powerless!

I only know how to release
the Brahmastra.

My father did not teach me
how to recall it.

VYASA: The sun shall be extinguished!
                    The earth shall become a wasteland
                    of ash and stones!

ASHWATTHAMA: Then listen to me, Vyasa.
                    Listen, Krishna.

                    The weapon
                    aimed at Uttara's womb
                    shall find its target.

                    It cannot be recalled!

(*There is a terrifying explosion.*)

VYASA: You are a beast!
                    You are a beast!
                    You are a beast!

(*Ashwatthama laughs wildly.*)

ASHWATTHAMA: I was not born a beast.
                    Yudhisthira made me one.

(*The stage up front is now fully lit. The lamentations of the widows of the Pandava soldiers become louder. Gandhari and Sanjaya enter.*)

GANDHARI: Keep walking, Sanjaya!
                    Who is wailing?
                    Can you hear them?

SANJAYA: Ashwatthama's Brahmastra
                    has destroyed the child
                    in Uttara's womb.

GANDHARI: He will fulfil his vow.
                    He will!

SANJAYA: (*After a pause*)

But, Gandhari
Krishna will
never forgive him.

GANDHARI: Do not stop, Sanjaya.

Krishna will never
be able to kill him.

Even if Krishna's disc
slices me into shreds
even then
I shall go to the place
where Duryodhana lies
in the sleep of death.

Let us go, Sanjaya.

(*They leave. Dhritarashtra and Yuyutsu enter.*)

DHRITARASHTRA: Son
let me grant you
my share of life
for you must live.

If Ashwatthama's Brahmastra
has destroyed the child
in Uttara's womb
then who knows
Yudhisthira may leave
the kingdom to you.

YUYUTSU: (*Laughing bitterly*)

And so
Ashwatthama's bestial act
may restore my lost inheritance.

No, Maharaj.

No.
Is my life not miserable enough!

(Shouts of victory from the Pandava camp. Vidura enters.)

DHRITARASHTRA: Who is rejoicing?

VIDURA: Krishna
                 has saved the child
                 in Uttara's womb!

DHRITARASHTRA: *(After a moment's silence)*

                 How, Vidura?

VIDURA: Krishna said:
                     'Let the Brahmastra
                     fall where it will.
                     I shall exchange my life
                     for Uttara's still-born child.'

DHRITARASHTRA: And did Krishna
                 spare Ashwatthama's life?

VIDURA: Yes, he spared him!
                 But after cursing him
                 for infanticide
                 and forcing him
                 to surrender
                 his talismanic gem ...

                 His talismanic gem
                 in exchange for his life
                 under the shadow of a curse forever.

                 And then
                 depressed
                 head bowed in defeat
                 Ashwatthama left.

YUYUTSU: I dread to think
                      what Gandhari
                      will do when she hears
                      of Ashwatthama's defeat.

DHRITARASHTRA: You go ahead
                      and find her.
                      I shall follow
                      as fast as I can.

(*Vidura leaves quickly. Dhritarashtra and Yuyutsu slowly follow. After a pause,
Sanjaya, Vidura, and Gandhari enter.*)

SANJAYA: This is the place.
                      This is the very spot where
                      Duryodhana fell.

                      Here is his golden helmet.
                      This is his club.
                      And there lies his armour.

(*Gandhari removes her blindfold. Touches each object. Takes the armour in her
arms and begins to mourn.*)

VIDURA: Endure this
                      with courage, Gandhari.
                      Armour can offer
                      no real protection.

                      Only virtuous actions
                      which man performs
                      by his own free will
                      can be his protection
                      his safety.

(*Gandhari suddenly looks off-stage and utters a cry of surprise.*)

GANDHARI: Who is that man
                      sitting in silence
                      next to the bush?
                      Is he alive?

VIDURA: Gandhari
                do not look at him!

GANDHARI: He looks like Ashwatthama!

SANJAYA: No, no!
                He is hideous.
                His body is covered
                with boils and open sores.

                He smells worse
                than a diseased dog!

GANDHARI: He is going away.
                Who is he, Vidura?
                Stop him!

VIDURA: He is Ashwatthama, Gandhari.
                Let him go.

                For the sin of infanticide
                Krishna has cursed him
                with immortality
                and condemned him
                to live forever and ever.

                Cut and slashed by the Lord's disc
                his body shall fester forever.
                Soiled bandages shall staunch
                the blood that shall flow
                from his wounds forever and ever.

                Lacerated, defiled, filthy, and corrupted
                he shall wander
                through thick and deep forests
                forever and ever.

                His body shall be covered with boils
                his skin shall fester with pus and scabs
                and spittle and phlegm and bile
                and he shall live forever and ever.

Excruciating pain will rip
through each limb.

Every bone in his body
will be corroded by suffering
but the Lord shall not let him die.

He will become an abomination
but he shall live forever and ever.

GANDHARI: Stop him, Sanjaya!
For his sake
I will challenge
Krishna today.

SANJAYA: He has gone.
Perhaps he had come
to pay his last respects
to these bones of Duryodhana.

GANDHARI: These bones?
Are they all
that remain
of my son?

VIDURA: Gandhari
be courageous.

GANDHARI: (*In a heart-rending voice*)

So
these bones
are all that remain
of my son!

What have you done, Krishna?
What have you done?

Hear me now!
You will have to hear me today!

Hear me, Gandhari
who has sacrificed everything
who has lived a virtuous life
who has lived a life of penance
and has earned the right
to tell you this:
    If you wanted
    you could have stopped the war.

I did not give birth
to this pile of bones.

You incited Bhima's adharma
but you inflicted
a vile curse on Ashwatthama
who had committed no crime!

    You used your divine power
    for unjust ends.

If my sacrifice has any meaning
if my penance has any sanction in dharma
then listen, Krishna, to what I have to say:

    You may be a god
    you may be omnipotent
    whatever you are
    whoever you are
    I curse you
    and I curse
    all your friends and kinsmen.
    They shall attack and kill each other.
    They shall eat each other
    like rabid dogs.

    And many years later
    after you have witnessed
    their destruction
    you will return to this forest
    only to be killed

like a wild animal
by an ordinary hunter!

(*Gentle sounds of a flute can be heard floating across the stage. The shadow of Krishna falls upon the rear wall of the stage.*)

KRISHNA: Mother.
I may be god.
I may be omnipotent.
But I am also your son
and you are my mother.

I said to Arjuna:
'I take upon my shoulders
the responsibility
of all your good and evil deeds.'

In this terrible war of eighteen days
I am the only one who died a million times.
Every time a soldier was struck down
every time a soldier fell to the ground
it was I who was struck down
it was I who was wounded
it was I who fell to the ground.

It is I who shall flow
in the pus
in the blood
in the spittle
that will ooze
out of Ashwatthama's body
from age to age
forever and ever.

If I am life
then, Mother
I am also death.

I accept your curse, Mother!

GANDHARI: O Krishna
what have you done!

(*Begins to weep loudly.*)

I did not weep like this
for my hundred sons.

O Krishna
as a mother
deep and profound
is my affection for you.

You could have refused
to accept my curse!

Had you done so
would I have grieved?

I was bitter
heart-broken and forlorn.

I had lost all my sons!

KRISHNA: No, Mother
do not say that.

I am alive
I may be a god
I may be omnipotent
but I am your son
and you are my mother.

GANDHARI: (*Weeping*)

Oh, what have I done, Vidura?
What have I done?

(*As the lights begin to dim, the Chorus begins its narration.*)

CHORUS: From the moment Krishna
accepted Gandhari's curse
the stars began to grow dim.

The word 'honour'
which had gathered meaning over ages
lost all value for the living.

Disenchanted poets
forgot to measure and scan their lines.

Everyone heard the curse
but no one had the courage
to speak to Gandhari.

Its corrosive shadow
spread from age to age
and stained every heart
and every soul
with sorrow.

ACT FIVE

Victory and a Series of Suicides

CHORUS:
Days and weeks
months and years passed by.

Scorched earth
slowly turned
green and fertile again.

Yudhishthira had finally won
his throne and his kingdom
but the old city of the Kauravas
never did regain its days of glory again.

The Pandavas were victorious
but their self-confidence was shattered.

Krishna was their guardian, their councillor
—the shaping spirit of their days—
but he himself was under a curse.

And so the Pandavas
who had founded their kingdom
on the ruins of war
began their confused and inauspicious reign
without the customary rites of virtue.

Bhima was proud by nature
and intellectually dull.

Arjuna had grown old and weary
before his time.

Nakula was ignorant
and Sahadeva retarded from birth.

Yudhishthira
his brow marked deep with sorrow
was the only one
who saw the future
as a nightmare.

Yudhishthira
was the only one
who understood
that when Krishna
—still under the shadow of the curse—
met with a violent death as prophesied
the days they had sown together
in the battlefield
would yield a harvest of such bitterness
that all the wisdom of past ages
would be covered with dust and darkness.

His head resting on his knees
lost in his own dark thoughts
Yudhishthira often sat
on the stone steps of the palace
and stared with vacant eyes
at the encroaching darkness.

(*The curtain rises. Two old guards stand at the back of the stage. Yudhishthira is sitting in the foreground.*)

YUDHISHTHIRA: What is the cause of my sorrow?

Though I won the war
a ferocious war
full of treachery
and bloodshed
and slaughter
I am alone
and defeated.

Those I had fought for
my kinsmen, my brothers, my family

are either ignorant or foolish
insolent or weary.

Behind the throne I won
stretches a long and unbroken
tradition of blindness and stupidity.

The people are still cast
in the ugly mould of the old regime.

I tremble
as I watch the encroaching darkness
and hear the sinister steps
of the coming age.

And yet
I must continue to live on
and wear in my crown
the jewel plucked
from the forehead of that murderer
Ashwatthama.

O Duryodhana
my brother
you are more fortunate than I am
for having left this world
before me.

I am alone
and defeated.

I sit here
and listen
to the sinister steps
of the coming age.

Whom can I warn?

My brothers
are either ignorant or foolish
insolent or weary.

(*The sound of loud and vulgar laughter is heard from the wings.*)

>   Perhaps
>   Bhima has insulted
>   someone again.

(*Bhima's wild laughter breaks in once again.*)

>   That is an example
>   of my family's grim humour.

>   In a few years
>   the surrounding darkness
>   shall swallow them all.

>   But who is enthralled
>   by Bhima's
>   insolent wit?

(*Sounds of applause and laughter off-stage. Vidura and Kripacharya enter in great agitation.*)

VIDURA: Maharaj
                Bhima has become intolerable.
                Who will stop his impudence?

YUDHISHTHIRA: What has he done this time, Vidura?

VIDURA: What he does everyday.

                He has humiliated Yuyutsu
                once again.

KRIPACHARYA: Encouraged
                the crowd mocks Yuyutsu
                for having lost his voice.

YUDHISHTHIRA: I wonder
                what has happened
                to Yuyutsu's voice.
                He cannot speak a word.

VIDURA: Over the years
                     he has endured
                     the hatred
                     of his family
                     and the insults
                     of the people of this city.

                     He was a devout worshipper
                     of Krishna
                     whose own life is now
                     under the shadow
                     of Gandhari's curse.

KRIPACHARYA: You gave Yuyutsu refuge.

                     But
                     Yuyutsu lost his power of speech
                     the day
                     Gandhari and blind Dhritarashtra
                     retired to the forest ashram
                     unable to bear
                     Bhima's angry taunts.

YUDHISHTHIRA: He has suffered much.

                     He alone dared to stand up
                     against his family
                     and risk his life.

                         But in the end
                         his faith was betrayed.

                     Constantly abused
                     he cannot even retaliate
                     like that brute
                     Ashwatthama.

(*Bhima roars again.*)

KRIPACHARYA: Maharaj

come and console
Yuyutsu yourself.

(Exit Yudhishthira, Vidura, and Kripacharya. The old guards walk up to the front of the stage.)

GUARD 1:   Some went mad.

GUARD 2:   Some were cursed.

GUARD 1:   Yet we remained …

GUARD 2:   as we always were.

GUARD 1:   The ruler changed …

GUARD 2:   … but the conditions remained the same.

GUARD 1:   The previous ruler was a better king.

GUARD 2:   He was blind …

GUARD 1:   … but at least he knew how to rule.
                    This one is a saint and a philosopher.

GUARD 2:   How can he rule?

GUARD 1:   He does not know
                    what his people are like.

GUARD 2:   Knowledge and morality …

GUARD 1:   what can we do with them?

GUARD 2:   Grind them?

GUARD 1:   Or eat them?

GUARD 2:   Wear them?

GUARD 1:   Or lie on them?

GUARD 2:   If only we had enough grain …

GUARD 1:   … clear instructions …

GUARD 2:   … a strong leader …

GUARD 1:   … and orders we could blindly follow …

GUARD 2:   … to wage war
                    or live in peace.

GUARD 1:   He does not know
                    what his people are like.

(*Enter Yuyutsu. The guards fall silent and retreat to their earlier positions. Yuyutsu makes incoherent attempts to speak, and then leaves in great agitation. A few moments later, Vidura and Kripacharya enter.*)

VIDURA: Have you seen Yuyutsu?

(*One of the guards points in the direction Yuyutsu had left.*)

KRIPACHARYA: His life is unfortunate.

                    He wanders through the city streets
                    aimlessly.

VIDURA: Has he not been
                    abused enough
                    in the palace?

                    Must he also wander
                    through the city streets
                    so that the people
                    can insult him?

KRIPACHARYA: Look!
                    Over there!

He is being followed
by a large crowd
of ragged children
and lame, deformed, mutilated
beggars.

They are taunting him!
Abusing him!

VIDURA: Oh no!
                     Someone has thrown
                     a stone at him!

(*Worried, he goes to help Yuyutsu.*)

KRIPACHARYA: Under Yudhishthira's reign
                     this is the fate of Yuyutsu
                     who upheld dharma!

(*Vidura enters supporting Yuyutsu. Yuyutsu's face is bleeding. Vidura wipes the
blood from Yuyutsu's face with the hem of his robe. The mute soldier who had
lost his voice follows them. He throws a stone at Yuyutsu and laughs wildly.*)

VIDURA: Guard
                     who let this beggar in here?

                     Yuyutsu, come with me.

(*The mute soldier indicates through gestures: 'He broke my legs. Why should I
not seek revenge?'*)

KRIPACHARYA: Yuyutsu broke only your legs
                     but today I shall break
                     every bone in your body
                     till you are dead.

(*Kripacharya grabs a spear from one of the soldiers and rushes towards the beggar
who turns and hobbles away. Yuyutsu restrains Kripacharya. Then Yuyutsu snatches
the spear from Kripacharya's hand and plunges it into his own heart. He staggers
off-stage. A terrifying scream is heard from the wings. Vidura runs after Yuyutsu.*)

VIDURA: (*Off-stage.*) Maharaj
Yuyutsu has committed suicide.

Help, Kripacharya!

(*Kripacharya leaves. The two old guards come forward.*)

GUARD 1: In war or in peace ...

GUARD 2: there is always bloodshed.

GUARD 1: If there are weapons ...

GUARD 2: they will be used.

GUARD 1: Till now
these weapons ...

GUARD 2: were raised
against our enemies.

GUARD 1: Now they will be used
against us.

GUARD 2: Our weapons
which were useless till now ...

GUARD 1: have at last served

GUARD 2: some purpose today!

(*Sounds of wild laughter off-stage. Kripacharya enters.*)

KRIPACHARYA: The brothers of Yudhishthira
are either foolish or ignorant
insolent or arrogant.

They even laugh at death!

They cannot decipher

what Yuyutsu wrote today
with his own blood
on this war-torn land.

His suicide shall leave its mark
on our entire civilization—
its philosophy, dharma, art
society and politics.

From now on
man shall work towards
his own destruction.

(*Vidura enters.*)

VIDURA: It is sometimes possible
for one who slaughters his own people
or murders his mother or his beloved
or kills women and children
to find his way to salvation.

But the one who kills himself
wanders like a haunted spirit
in realms of darkness
forever and ever.

KRIPACHARYA: And that shall be
the fate of Yuyutsu.

Today
in this magnificent palace of Yudhishthira
I can hear the ominous footsteps
of a future age.

I only agreed to stay here
All these years
to teach Parikshit
the art of war.

But Yudhishthira's kingdom
is decadent
and cowardly.
It is bent upon its own
destruction.

I must leave
Hastinapur at once.

That would be the wisest thing to do.

Self-destruction
is a fatal disease
which spreads
like an epidemic.

VIDURA: But you are a brahmin ...

KRIPACHARYA: No! No!

I was a soldier once.

I can no longer live
in Yudhishthira's kingdom.

It is bent upon
its own annihilation.

VIDURA: In Yudhishthira's kingdom
people will commit suicide.
Brahmins will seek protection.

O Lord
what kind of peace
have you given us!

What will happen
when Dhritarashtra
in his forest ashram
learns of Yuyutsu's death?

(*Yudhishthira enters.*)

YUDHISHTHIRA: There is still some life
                     left in Yuyutsu.

VIDURA: If he is still alive
                     send him to my hut.
                     I shall protect him
                     nurse him.

                     It shall be a small recompense
                     for all he has suffered
                     in Krishna's cause ...

(*Yudhishthira and Vidura leave. The lights become dim.*)

GUARD 1:   Why has it suddenly become dark?

GUARD 2:   There are clouds of smoke over the forest!

GUARD 1:   The forest is ablaze!

(*The guards leave. We catch a glimpse of Sanjaya and Dhritarashtra surrounded by flames. The entire stage is slowly filled with the glow of the forest fire.*)

DHRITARASHTRA: Let it be, Sanjaya.

                     You shall not be able
                     to save me today.

                     I am old and feeble.
                     How far can I run
                     from the fire?

SANJAYA: There is a shelter
                     not far from here.
                     Let us go there, Maharaj.

(*Turns to look back.*)

                     Oh, Gandhari has collapsed!

Hurry, Gandhari!
Hurry!

DHRITARASHTRA: Sanjaya
all this effort
is now futile.

Leave me here.

I am old and blind.

All my life
I have wandered
in darkness.

Now I feel
as if the flames
have surrounded me
in a circle of light
and I am free.

All my life
I refused to see
the truth.

Let me feel the truth today
and wear it
on these aged bones
like a garland
of glowing embers.

SANJAYA: The fire is spreading.

Oh, no
Gandhari is
surrounded by the flames!

I am helpless!
I cannot save them both.

(*Gandhari enters. She is badly burnt.*)

GANDHARI: Please leave
Sanjaya.

        All this
        is the result
           of my curse
           on Krishna.

        Suicide
        violence
        adharma
        and family strife
        have grown
        a hundredfold
        and infected
        all the cities and forests.

        Sanjaya
        tell Krishna:
           I was the first victim
           of my own curse.

(*Someone from the wings calls: 'Gandhari'.*)

DHRITARASHTRA: Oh no!
Kunti has been left behind
in the forest!
Let us turn back
Gandhari.

SANJAYA: Maharaj
Maharaj
the fire is fierce.
Its countless flames
must have consumed
Kunti by now.

                    Maharaj
                    you are safe here.
                    Do not go.

GANDHARI: Sanjaya
                    let those who have
                    spent their lives
                    wandering in darkness
                    at last die
                    in the fatal light
                    of this fire.

(She takes Dhritarashtra by the hand and turns to walk towards the burning forest. Sanjaya watches them helplessly.)

SANJAYA: Oh, no!
                    A banyan tree
                    in a blaze of fire
                    has fallen on them.

                    Now
                    I am the only one
                    left alive.

                    I am alone
                    utterly alone.

                    My life is meaningless.

                    Why am I alive?
                    Why should I
                    continue to live?

(A burning branch of a tree falls on his foot. In agony, he clutches his foot and sits down. The curtain falls.)

CHORUS: Thus the reign of the Pandava kingdom came to
                    an end.

                    Day by day Yudhishthira grew increasingly dejected

Slowly he lost faith in everything
hope in everything
and in the ever-increasing darkness
understood that his victory in war was hollow.

(*The two old guards enter. Yudhishthira's crown is stuck on the spear of one of the guards.*)

GUARD 1:   This is the crown
                      of the mighty king.

GUARD 2:   Wear it!
                      He put it aside ...

GUARD 1:   when he saw signs of evil
                      in the city of Hastinapur.

GUARD 2:   Quick
                      Maharaj Yudhishthira
                      is coming this way.

(*Yudhishthira and Vidura enter.*)

VIDURA: These are signs
                      of evil.

                      They carry
                      the prophecy ...

YUDHISHTHIRA: Of Krishna's death!

                      I know.

                      Messengers from all over
                      have brought me news
                      of increasing strife
                      amidst the Yadava clan.

VIDURA: Send Arjuna
                      at once to Dwarkapuri.

YUDHISHTHIRA: Vidura
                  what shall I do?

                  Dhritarashtra, Gandhari
                  and Kunti were burnt to ash
                  in that terrible fire.

                  Yuyutsu's wounds reopened
                  when he performed the last rites.
                  He has finally succeeded
                  in committing suicide.
                  I could not save his life.

                  Have I alone
                  been condemned
                  to witness Lord Krishna's death?

                  No, no!
                  Let me go!
                  Let my body
                  slowly decay
                  on some Himalayan slope.

VIDURA: Maharaj
                  that too would be suicide.

                  Even the height of those slopes
                  will not redeem
                  such a sinful
                  and cowardly act.

                  For to seek
                  a slow death
                  on some Himalayan peak
                  would still be suicide.

YUDHISHTHIRA: And what is
                  victory then?
                  Is that not also
                  a long and slow act
                  of suicide?

No, there is no other path
left open to me.

(They leave as they talk. The old guards come forward.)

GUARD 1: Every day there is a new omen
of evil times to come.

GUARD 2: Yesterday
it rained
rocks and stones.

GUARD 1: Today
you can see
dark and headless corpses
dance in the sun.

GUARD 2: I have heard
that the destruction of Krishna—
the one whom they call Lord—
is at hand.

GUARD 1: It is said
that Yamaraj—
in black and yellow robes—
walks through the streets
of Dwarkapuri
at midnight.

GUARD 2: And that renowned archers
rain arrows at him.
But
whirling like a cyclonic storm
he suddenly vanishes.

GUARD 1: And that
the one they call
Lord ...

GUARD 2: the one who was
supposed to bear

the burden of their well being
on his shoulders ...

GUARD 1:   shall soon
                  abandon them
                  here on earth
                  without a path
                  without a goal ...

GUARD 2:   and return
                  to his own abode.

GUARD 1:   Impoverished and abandoned
                  what shall they do now?

GUARD 2:   Compared to them
                  the two of us
                  are better off!

GUARD 1:   We have not faced grief ...

GUARD 2:   nor endured pain.

GUARD 1:   We are now ...

GUARD 2:   as we always were!

EPILOGUE

Death of the Lord

INVOCATION:

You are the word, O Lord!
You are the meaning of meaning.

You are our refuge, O Lord!
You are our consolation.

Those who cry out to you, O Lord
never cry in vain!

We sing in your praise, O Lord!
We sing in praise of your devotees, O Lord
devotees who have sung in your praise
from generation to generation
about the mysteries of your acts
the mysteries of your creation.

Grant this lonely pilgrim
in search of faith, O Lord
a few words, a few thoughts, a few images
to sing in sorrow at your sacrificial death!

CHORUS:

It was a radiant forest
by the shore of the sea.
Sun-kissed waves crashed against the sands
sea-washed breezes swept through the palm trees
the fragrance of tulsi filled the forest air with
sweetness.

Under the shade of a peepul tree
Lord Krishna sat on the cool earth
calm, silent, still, and at peace.

His body, dark as the clouds
seemed a little tired, a little weary

the last petal on a lotus
in a garland of flowers.

Shadows of peepul leaves
played on his gracious forehead.

Heavy with sleep
his eyelids drooped
like the half-open petals
of a blue lotus.

He leaned against the tree
placed his left foot
shaped like a deer's face
on his right thigh
and with a sigh whispered:
'A strange age has passed.'

(*Lights. Ashwatthama, who looks like a terrifying beast, enters.*)

ASHWATTHAMA: That song of praise is false.
                    Those words of homage are false.

                    Krishna acted
                    as I did in the Pandava camp.

                        The one who dreams
                        and the one who is intoxicated
                        are the same.

                    He slaughtered
                    all his kinsmen
                    who were drunk.

                    I recently saw
                    with my own eyes
                    countless
                    dark and blood-stained bodies
                    of Yadava soldiers

scattered on the glittering sands
of the ocean shore.

They had been killed
by Krishna himself.

He acted
as I did that night.

The only difference was
that I killed my enemies
while he slaughtered
his own kinsmen.

He sits there
under the ashwatha tree
powerless, dejected and tired.

I shall ask him
why my body
is tormented
by the pain of infinite hells
while his lotus-like body
has not been corroded
by a thousand wounds
and a thousand sores.

(Exit Ashwatthama. Sanjaya enters. He drags himself onto the stage.)

SANJAYA: I had once told you, O Lord:
                              even if
                              I did not have arms
                              I would still embrace you

                              even if
                              I did not have eyes
                              I would still gaze upon you

                              even if
                              I did not have legs

I would still
find you!

But today, O Lord
my pride is shattered.

All my life I upheld my faith
in the absolute Truth.

I refused to act.

Slowly I lost my divine vision.

And that day
in the forest inferno
even my legs were
badly singed.

(*A hunter enters and crouches behind a bush. He takes aim with his bow and arrow.*)

CHORUS: (*Singing softly*)

In the distance
under the shadow
of a thorny bush
a hunter crouches.

Mistaking
Krishna's foot for a deer
he draws his bowstring
and takes aim.

SANJAYA: (*Suddenly noticing the hunter*)

Stop! Stop!
Oh! He cannot hear me.

A divine radiance

shall soon be extinguished
from our world.

I have dragged myself across
hundreds of miles
but I will never reach
that *ashwatha* tree.

(*The hunter releases his arrow. There is a flash of lightning. Three sharp notes of a flute are heard. As they fade away, Ashwatthama laughs wildly. Sanjaya screams and faints. Darkness.*)

CHORUS: The stars went out
                         darkness covered the earth
                         and that forest of fear
                         . became even more terrifying.

                     The moment Krishna was killed
                         Dvapara yug came to an end
                         and on this god-forsaken earth
                         Kali yug took its first step.

                         And that forest of fear
                             became even more terrifying.

(*Ashwatthama enters.*)

ASHWATTHAMA: I was the only witness
                     to Krishna's death.

                     I hid behind the palm trees.
                     Their leaves
                     sharper than a sword's edge
                     cut into my putrefied flesh.
                     But I held my breath
                     and stood there transfixed
                     without uttering a sound.

(*Deeply aggrieved*)

When the arrow pierced him
I was surprised to see
his foot blister
as my body does—
the same dark blood
flow out of his foot
as from my festering wounds.

Listen
Krishna
you are my enemy.

But tell me:
When you died
did you give
this brute Ashwatthama
sanctuary at your feet?

Did your blood
atone for me?

When poison
oozes out of a boil
the body ceases to feel pain.

In the same way
I now feel relief
from past suffering.

Is this experience
the beginning of faith?

Is this experience
faith?

YUYUTSU: (*Speaking off-stage.*)

Whose voice do I hear
in these dark times?

Who has discovered
faith once more?

That brute
Ashwatthama?

(*Laughs loudly.*)

Faith is a worn-out coin.
Has Ashwatthama found it now?

I discovered it was false
and counterfeit
a long time ago
and threw it away
on a garbage heap.

SANJAYA: That is Yuyutsu's voice!
He is doomed to wander
like a blind soul
in this vast universe.

(*Yuyutsu enters. He gropes his way, like a blind spirit, to the front of the stage.*)

YUYUTSU: I have heard the news
of my damnation:
'You took your own life.
You are doomed
to wander aimlessly
through dark worlds.'

Is there a place darker than the earth?

I was born to a blind king.

For a few years
I was deluded
by my faith
in Krishna's false dharma.

But
I committed suicide
and broke the adamantine
doors of death
only to find myself
once again
in the caves of darkness.

I too have come to witness
the epiphany of Krishna's death.

Alive
he failed
to kindle faith in us.

Now he has enacted
the drama of his death
to enslave us.

I think
he was a coward
and an imposter.

He was also impotent
for he could neither save Parikshit
nor save me.

He has returned
to his own kingdom.

In this blind age
whenever the future
is threatened
by a Brahmastra
a venomous snake
shall bite Parikshit
and many a Yuyutsu
shall be driven to suicide.

Who will come to their rescue?
Will you, Ashwatthama?

You are immortal
are you not?

ASHWATTHAMA: But I am that monstrous half-truth
reduced to a wild beast
who hates everything.

YUYUTSU: And you, Sanjaya?
You are a believer.

SANJAYA: But I am the upholder
of the absolute Truth.

I remain neutral.

I can neither kill
nor save.

Far removed
from the field of action
I have slowly forgotten
the meaning
of existence.

YUYUTSU: That is why
I proclaim boldly
that our fate is linked
not to the death of Krishna
but to the future of mankind!
To the survival of Parikshit!

How will he be saved?
That is my concern.

How can he be saved?

I ask as one
who has suffered contempt
for Krishna's sake
all his life.

Is there no one left
who has faith enough
to give me an answer?

(*The old mendicant, with a bow in his hand, enters.*)

MENDICANT: I am still here
                  to give you an answer.

YUYUTSU: Who are you?
                  I cannot see you clearly.

MENDICANT: Now I am an old hunter.
                  My name is Jara.
                  It was the arrow from my bow
                  that killed Krishna.

                  Earlier
                  I was the old astrologer.

                  Ashwatthama killed me.

                  To free my soul
                  from this spectral world
                  Krishna said to me:
                      'It is now time
                      for Gandhari's curse
                      to be fulfilled.
                      Pick up your bow
                      and shoot the arrow.'

                  I was filled with dread.
                  But he reassured me:
                      'Ashwatthama committed a sin
                      by killing you.

I shall atone for it
through my suffering.

My death shall free you
from this spectral world.'

ASHWATTHAMA: The sin was mine.
I killed you.

But the hands that killed you
were not mine.
The heart that killed you
was not mine.

The blindness of this age
flowed through my veins.

In my madness
I sought revenge.
In my ignorance
I sought vengeance.

The one whom you call Lord
was my enemy
but he took
even my sufferings
upon himself.

My body is still covered
with wounds
but I feel no pain.
I am condemned
yet free!

YUYUTSU: Perhaps
his death has atoned
for the crimes of murderers
and set them free.

After Krishna's

cowardly murder
who will save man
in dark times?

ASHWATTHAMA: Cowardly murder?

He was my enemy.

Yet I know that
when he died
a peaceful radiance
spread over his face—
a divinity
and a grace.

MENDICANT: At the last moment of his life
the Lord said to me:
'O aged hunter
death does not exist.
Death is only a transition
from one state to another.

I took upon myself
the burdens of everyone.

Now all those who live
must assume these burdens.

Till now I made sure
that human life endured.
But in this blind age
a part of me
will always be
degraded
mutilated
or destroyed
like Sanjaya or Yuyutsu or Ashwatthama—
because I have taken their sins upon myself.'

He added:

'Yet there will be others
many others
who shall have
faith in me
and with that faith
in their hearts
find their way
past every difficulty.
They shall build a new life
on the ruins of the old.

Honourable in their conduct
imaginative in their actions
fearless
courageous
affectionate
joyful
they shall find me
present
again and again
in every moment
of their lives.'

ASHWATTHAMA: Given this new meaning of Krishna's presence
can the life
of a crude and coarse man—
however disfigured or barbaric
ferocious or faithless—
be redeemed?

MENDICANT: Yes! Certainly!

He is the future.
You hold Him in your hands.

Whenever you like
you can destroy Him.

Whenever you like
you can make Him

a radiant presence
in your life.

SANJAYA: But
                      I am deformed
                      and paralysed.

ASHWATTHAMA: And
                      I have become a beast.

YUYUTSU: And
                      I am the blind spirit
                      of a man who killed himself.

(*The old mendicant steps forward. All the other characters slowly step back. The curtain in the middle drops. The light now is only on the old mendicant. The rest of the stage is in darkness.*)

MENDICANT: They are dejected
                      and blind
                      and paralysed
                      and monstrous
                      and the darkness
                      grows deeper and deeper.

                      Will someone
                      who is not blind
                      who is not deformed
                      listen to me
                      and be the saviour
                      of the future of man?

                          I am Jara
                          the old hunter.
                          I was the instrument
                          of His metamorphosis.

                          I heard the last
                          dying words
                          of the Lord.

With raised hands
I repeat them
again and again.

Listen to me!

Is there anyone
who will listen to me?

Is there anyone
who will listen to me?

(*As the lights begin to dim, the Chorus steps forward.*)

CHORUS: That day the world descended into the age of
darkness
which has no end, and repeats itself over and over
again.
Every moment the Lord dies somewhere or the
other
every moment the darkness grows deeper and
deeper.

The age of darkness has seeped into our very souls.

There is darkness, and there is Ashwatthama, and
there is Sanjaya
and there are the two old guards with the mentality
of slaves
and there is blind doubt, and a shameful sense of
defeat.

And yet it is also true
that like a small seed
buried somewhere
in the mind of man
there is courage
and a longing for freedom
and the imagination to create something new.

That seed is buried
without exception
in each of us
and it grows from day to day
in our lives
as duty
as honour
as freedom
as virtuous conduct.

It is this small seed
that makes us fear
half-truths
and great wars
and always
saves
the future of mankind
from blind doubt
slavery
and defeat.

THE END